DATE DUE

AUG 2 4 1991			
JUN 3 1992			

HIGHSMITH 45-220

MOVING PICTURES
Their Impact on Society

A facsimile reprint collection

JEROME S. OZER Publisher
1971

Advisory Editor: GARTH S. JOWETT

Library of Congress Catalog Card No. 72-160230

Manufactured in the United States of America

CENSORED

JONATHAN CAPE AND HARRISON SMITH, INCORPORATED, 139 EAST 46TH STREET, NEW YORK, N. Y. AND 77 WELLINGTON STREET, WEST, TORONTO, CANADA; JONATHAN CAPE, LTD., 30 BEDFORD SQUARE, LONDON, W. C. 1, ENGLAND

"THE PATRIOT." Passed in Germany, on Broadway, and
at the corner bookstore. Not in Pennsylvania.
One of the many cuts.

CENSORED

THE PRIVATE LIFE
OF THE MOVIE

BY
MORRIS L. ERNST
AND
PARE LORENTZ

NEW YORK
JONATHAN CAPE AND HARRISON SMITH

FOREWORD

MUCH of the onslaught against censorship of all kinds has been conducted by crusaders saying, "We do not believe in any sort of censorship at any time." That is a fine, brave stand and a logical one as well, but unfortunately not always true. Even the most advanced thinker can generally be affrighted by some obscene display to such a point that he will abandon his principles and admit, "Well, yes, that I would suppress." Only very staunch souls are capable of living up to the Voltairean slogan. We do not really wish to die for opinions which we despise.

I am myself a member of the school which asks for the abolition of all censorship. Yet I will admit that I can be backed into corners where certain exhibits worry me.

Moreover, I am aware that very many people do not wish to go to the length of granting complete freedom even to blatant obscenity. It is not unreasonable that some common ground should be found for an alliance between those who fight censorship on principle and the much greater number who oppose merely its follies. After all it would be a little academic to protest against a censorship so liberal that it simply remained in office and never deleted anything. Even the stalwarts, I think, would not be violently passionate against a censorship carried on by a little group composed of the wisest persons in the world. If unable to get my motion pictures and talkies straight, I would not be wholly incensed to receive only such films as were licensed by Havelock Ellis and John Dewey.

Of course, some have argued that a stupid censorship is better than a wise one since fools will soon destroy themselves. This might be true if the cutting were done openly but most of us are quite unaware of what has been taken out of the picture which we witness in its garbled form. Censorship is not the whole trouble. Part of it is the censors.

Pare Lorentz and Morris L. Ernst have

written a book which is decidedly practical as well as fascinating. In *Censored: The Private Life of the Movies* they have revealed to what I hope will be a startled public, the individual incapacity of the men and women who have been put in control of the destinies of a potentially great art.

And it seems to me that all those who believe in freedom of expression should make the motion pictures their chief concern. Much protest gets into print about slights and bans placed upon the drama. There should be roaring and tumult when *Strange Interlude* is banished out of Boston but it is well to remember that the so-called legitimate theatre now plays a very small part in the communal life of America. It is an art restricted to the very few. The motion picture shares with the newspaper and the radio the honour of being the most influential factor in moulding public opinion. In fact I doubt if any successful reform can be effected if a place upon the screen is definitely denied to its propagandists.

The utter reactionary quality of motion picture censorship in the United States is

FOREWORD

shown in *Censored*. Obviously politicians of
the lowest order have been made the guardians of public morals. Anyone who fails to
read the book will miss the massing of a most
engrossing indictment, but I almost believe
that the authors could prove their case by
doing no more than print the portraits of the
men and women who have been set in the high
seats and commissioned to frame the taste of
the entire picture-going world.

HEYWOOD BROUN.

CONTENTS

ILLUSTRATIONS

INTRODUCTION

A LAWYER and a movie critic were discussing the movies. The lawyer was familiar with some of their trials; the critic their tribulations. Neither of us could understand why the American movie, with all its power and promise, still lay in such a wallow of stupidity.

"The producers are illiterate" we said. But we knew some producers of real wit.

"The directors are yes-men; morons;" we had read many times. But we knew stage directors of worth who had gone West with real ability, and returned empty-handed. We said there must be other, deep-seated, reasons. We then discovered the movie censor. It was no easy task. Despite the enormous censorship machinery of the industry, the press, movie executives and the Hays office either knew nothing or would divulge no real information about the censors.

INTRODUCTION

Who are they? Why? How much do they make? Are they important? With the kindly support of the *Baltimore Sun* and a few real newspapers, and after several months of investigation by the movie critic, we were able to assemble something that looked like the machine that makes movies. Other writers might continue after us and consider such things as art and the movies' ultimate place in the sun. But until you know the unseen masters of the movies it is useless to discuss them in terms of art.

We put the censors—and words and photographs that are illegal to them—on paper, added them together and endeavoured to find the sum importance. We started at the bottom —Kansas—and worked to the top—Wall Street. We may have skipped a few stations on the way but we have given you an accurate account of a side-show in the biggest circus the world has ever known.

PROLOGUE

A GREAT barn-like building. Cranes, scenery, men and women idling under the glare of huge lights, their faces sickly with greasepaint. It is a movie set. Time: 1930. A bell rings. Silence! Lights! Camera! Action! They are filming a last season's stage success. The two perspiring actors struggle to register love and affection and close into a sticky embrace. He kisses her on the neck, leaving a faint impress of make-up.

"Cut."

The supervisor has stepped in.

"You can't do that."

The scenario writer reaches for a cigarette.

"Why not, in heaven's name?"

"It won't get by the Maryland board."

"But," protests the director, "it's right here in the script. This guy is in love with another man's wife. He's going away to China, going

for good. You don't think he'd just tip his hat,
do you? Call Colonel Joy."

The scenario writer gets the Colonel on the
wire. The supervisor is right. Maryland and
probably Pennsylvania would cut the long kiss.
The Colonel suggests that the bed be removed
from the scene and the fatal embrace cut to a
three-foot flash.

Again the bell tolls. Camera! Action! The
bedless masterpiece once more is under way.

BABY NEEDS STOCKINGS

I

Who is Colonel Joy?

Who comprises the "Maryland Board?"

What have they to do with movies?

With Democrats, Republicans, Jews, Greeks, movie fans, and movie scoffers?

These questions we have answered. Hated, despised, powerful and afraid, the movie business is a furious scramble of quacks, artists, and financiers. The technical difficulties, the financial involutions and the extraordinary personalities all deserve calm classification. But we have recognized a familiar scent among the many evil and exotic odours hanging over Hollywood and have attempted to condense and clarify this one only; a mysterious and important element that is included in the movie spirit.

Our frenzied scramble for production and wealth has produced no phenomenon as bewildering as the movie industry, the nation's fifth largest business. Untold wealth and untold influence have come out of the mad houses of Hollywood. The movie actor and the movie producer are American folk heroes. The one a Paris, a super-lover; the other a Maecenas; a king of uncounted wealth. Even the real men in the business cannot explain nor knit together the many tangled threads of life that hang to the ever-flowing stream of celluloid belting the world.

The movie was created, tried and developed in America. Supported by the dumb and the quick, rich and poor, it is the most powerful medium for news, opinion and art in the world. One important group of people associated with the business has escaped the eye of the press and the hand of the press agent. In the opening scene we gave you some idea of how close to the factory this group works.

2

BABY NEEDS STOCKINGS

We intend to show you the habits, the work, the power of this group: the movie censors.

The movie censor represents a peculiar relationship to the public, the artist, the financier. Above all, he offers as entertaining a show as can be seen in the complex currents of American life. The spectacle of an office full of men and women, hired (or self-appointed, as is many times the case), bending diligently to the task of finding smut, corruption, filth as their daily work, would be hilariously funny did they not hold the whip hand over the greatest artists, writers and actors of the land. What manner of people are these? Do they live the monastic lives of the Passion Players, or are they reformed crooks, evil livers turned to the good life, ably fitted to detect crime-inspiring words, lust-producing photographs?

There are state, federal and city movie censors. There are self-appointed censors, often asserting more power than the state-paid guardians of the pure. While they have no rules, no codified laws for determining what is pure, what is wicked, they work with the same technique from California to Maine.

3

PRIVATE LIFE OF THE MOVIE

Many people are not aware that such persons exist; that every screen exhibition is under the absolute tyranny of these mysterious potentates. Your newspaper reaches you fresh from the press room. Your magazine comes to your table with no more sanctification than the editor and the Post Office department choose to give it. The stage has its censors but with the exception of Boston and Philadelphia, they are not given first choice. They must wait until the public has passed judgment and then take their censure to the courts. But the movie goes through one purifying room to another.

It may be that the movie is a lost art, as useless to mankind—certainly to an American adult—as a fingernail. It is true that a peculiar association of circumstances has made it possible for an obscure minority to direct and repress the movie to an unbelievable extent.

It may be true that the actual work of this group is of no importance. The masses made the movie. It is a nationalism, a sectionalism of thought, desire, frustration, written large. Possibly the elimination of all censorship in the world would not save one soul, nor release

"SADIE THOMPSON." The occupation of the villain, Reverend Davidson, had to be changed for the sake of the censors. Even so, Mr. Barrymore and Miss Swanson had their work cut by several boards.

by one measure man's bewilderment. Yet a fanatic is a positive force. He is active. It happens that fanaticism reaches an epitome of organization in movie censorship. The movie censor is a curious exhibit, not only because he has flagellated life and courage from a promising craft, but because he has gained strength and has the dignity of law, salary, mothers and churches by his side. Before we have left the reviewing stand we shall see many familiar faces. Their numbers, the strength of their troops should not be underestimated.

Given a sheet of paper and a pen, a man is comparatively free to say what he likes. He is in an Eden of fair play compared to a director with a camera. Not the producer, not the public, nor even a small part of the public is responsible for the sterility of the American movie. Nor can the producer alone be blamed for the gross, vapid illusions of life contained in the ordinary movie. The censor, the forces giving him power, are responsible. We shall talk with him, work with him and see him. Meantime examine a few scattered examples of his work.

The play "Rain" was produced as "Sadie Thompson." The villain was a minister; in the movies he was reincarnated as a "professional reformer." Somerset Maugham, a writer and physician known and respected by intelligent people of three continents, wrote a story called "Miss Thompson." It was a story of a prostitute who was "saved" by a sex-starved evangelist, and then violated by her saviour who erased his sin by cutting his throat. The story was laid in the tropics; it was a psychological story of sex inhibition. It was no new topic, but the story was dramatized into a play called "Rain" and played for three years in the leading cities of the country.

In every nation this subject has served as a dramatic theme. "The Scarlet Letter" and "An American Tragedy," two best-selling novels of two different generations, touched upon this idea. "Hell Bent for Heaven," a prize-winning play by a Columbia professor, "Salvation," "Bride of the Lamb," "Revolt" and a host of plays and novels dealing with the physical relationship of sex and religion have appeared unmolested from time to time and from year

6

to year in this country. Yet "Rain" changed its name and the profession of its villain so that it could escape houndings by the censors. Fortunately, audiences could go to any corner bookstore and buy the original story and play, and fill in the gaps sliced by the censors. It is also worthy of note that Gloria Swanson, an old star, owns stock in the company that produced this dire and sinister movie; otherwise it is doubtful that it would ever have reached the screen.

In the movie "Old San Francisco" the heroine is kidnapped by a Chinaman and sold in the white slave traffic. Just as the villain is giving thanks to Buddha, the San Francisco earthquake intervenes to save her, thus explaining a catastrophe that cost many lives. "Old San Francisco" was not censored because it satisfied the one great tenet of the movie censors: "God is a force in the world that moves to preserve Christian virginity."

One of the most salacious scenes ever put into a film occurred in "The Prodigal," a dramatization of the Biblical legend. Practically all this movie contained was magnificent por-

7

trayals of the prodigal wasting his substance in riotous living. In one scene the temptress, barely covered by a leopard skin, receives the prodigal on a rose-strewn couch in no mild manner. Yet, because the hero was chastened, punished, and repented (in one short reel), this movie was hardly touched by the hands of the godly.

Nita Naldi appeared practically naked, whiskey and debauchery went on merrily in "The Ten Commandments," but because Cecil DeMille showed the Almighty putting on an electrical Fourth of July to put the fear of God into Moses, with subsequent death dealt to all sinners, the censors let this outrageous exhibition of bad taste slip by with little but words of praise and holy blessings.

Mary Pickford's talking movie, "Coquette," had to be entirely re-written because producers were told that the censors would not allow the heroine to be shown pregnant. We now come to serious tyranny. "Coquette" was a beautiful, dignified, drama. It was a heart-breaking story of a Southerner of the old school who caused the death of two youngsters who loved earnest-

8

"COQUETTE." Despite Miss Pickford's objection, the heroine could not be shown pregnant. "The censors would cut it" said the producers.

ly, simply because they defied the old school code of honour. There was not the slightest suggestion of vulgarity or indecency in one line of dialogue. Some of the lines were taken verbatim from the court testimony of a famous trial in South Carolina several years ago based on the same tragic situation. The play was written, in part, by one of the ablest men in the theatre, George Abbot. Helen Hayes, one of the most gracious and charming young actresses on the stage, played the leading role. The play hinged on the circumstance that the girl was with child by the man whom her father murdered. The dead man was killed by the father because he asked to marry the girl. The girl, in order to save her father from the disgrace which he did not know was imminent, committed suicide.

This is an unfair analysis of a very strong and beautiful play. The point is, the censor-conscious producer would not allow the movie to show the girl *enceinte,* thus destroying the whole plot.

The movie censor not only maintains the mortifying law-breaking habits of the old saloon-wreckers, but he also observes rigidly the fundamental characteristics of sex. To the movie censor love must end in marriage. His reasoning cannot attain a higher complexity.

In "Variety," the famous German movie that brought Emil Jannings to this country, the censors, New York excepted, cut out almost two reels, destroying the plot completely.

There is a humiliating attitude held by the entire movie control group. The papers, the novels, the books you read are published in large cities, as a rule, but they depend upon the support of all well-informed people everywhere. Movie producers, highly uninformed as to the real character of small towns, allow censors to badger them into cutting out "sex" scenes in films bound for the provinces. If the "sex" scene is just a Gilbert-Garbo necking party, then art and audiences have suffered no loss. If, on the other hand, it is a restrained dramatic situation such as was introduced in the first reel of "Variety," its loss destroys the meaning of the whole plot. Eighth Avenue day labourers in New York City could see "Variety" as it was made by its directors, but

10

BABY NEEDS STOCKINGS

the faculty and students of Lawrence, Kansas,
or Fayetteville Arkansas, could not!

The ruthless treatment of "Variety" was one
of the most mortifying scourgings ever given
a dignified work of art. Not only was this German picture an exhibition of the finest art of
the movie, but it was characterized by one of
the greatest German actors, Emil Jannings. In
this story the motivation of the tragedy was
carefully built in the first reel. A homely carnival trouper has a longing to return to the
circus as a trapeze actor. He and his wife had
once been star acrobats, a severe fall reducing
them to the cheap and unskilled occupation of
carnival workers. The longing for the circus
roof so haunts the carnival trouper that he allows one of his dancing girls to tear him from
his wife and child. The director took great
care to show the big fellow's love for his wife
and child; the Eurasian girl who takes him
away represents, first of all, a means of enjoy-
ing his love for the acrobatic bars, rather than
an experiment in illicit love.

Thus, when he has left his wife and child
and been at once servant, trainer and lover to

11

the girl, you can understand him killing the man who takes her from him. The sheer beauty of the photography alone made "Variety" an extraordinarily fine movie. No healthy normal man or woman could have detected the slightest note of vulgarity in its portrayal. It was human, earthy tragedy. Yet the censors in every state, with the exception of New York and a few cities, cut it almost to pieces. They cut out the first reel entirely, thus destroying the motivation of the tragedy, implying that the acrobat was married to his Eurasian temptress.

From the treatment given "Variety" you can easily understand why it is almost impossible to produce a great movie in this country. There is no such word in the censor's vocabulary as "taste."

It is maddening to realize that in our most prosperous age these little men are jerking us back into the dark ages of art. Even in Philadelphia—the home of the Curtis School of Music, the Academy of Art, the city of Joseph Pennell, Josef Hoffman, Leopold Stokowski—the censors made "Anna Karenina," heroine of Tolstoy's masterpiece, marry her lover; and

12

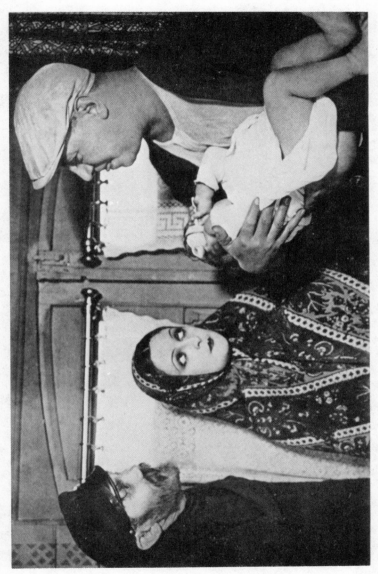

"VARIETY." Lya de Putti and Emil Jannings in a scene in the first reel. This reel was rejected *in toto* by practically every censor board.

destroyed the story of a philosopher respected by two generations.

Despite its childish extravaganza the movie of today is capable of producing adult entertainment. There are too many cheap novels, true story magazines, and tabloid newspapers in existence for the movie to bear the blame of mass expression. At its worst it is illiterate and childish. At its best, it is America's greatest contribution to art. Yet, at its best, it is unable to escape the unlearned and stupid hecklings of the censors. At its logical development, it could dwarf the stage, the press, and literature with its power. Let us look at the men at the throttle.

THE SAINTS AT WORK

II

Six STATES have movie censor boards:
New York, Pennsylvania, Maryland, Kansas,
Virginia, and Ohio. The laws creating these
boards were passed when the movie was of no
financial importance. In those days they were
fighting for patents, scrambling for money and
customers. If censorship meant more customers, then, hurrah for censorship! Nobody, not
even the producers, seriously cared or thought
of the consequences. For that matter, Edison
sold the British rights to his movie patents for
practically nothing.

In 1915, stage stars were ashamed to work
for the movies. Today, movie stars condescend

to make personal appearances; yet the censor born in 1911 has grown as quickly and has become as strong as the industry that feeds him.

Now, in 1930, whether we like it or not, the movie is a potent influence. And by an unchallenged circumstance, a man or woman whom you have never seen or even heard of has the power to say "you can't see that," or "you can't hear that."

Six states have censor boards.

"Then," you might conclude, "any kind of movies can get into the other 42 states." A state license may be approved by a neighbour state. That is, West Virginia usually gets movies cut by the Pennsylvania Board; Missouri, those cut and passed by Kansas, etc. Remember, too, that a few companies make 90% of our movies, 40% of the world's yearly exhibition. To make a movie costs from $35,000 to $1,500,000. At any rate, these companies spend that much, consequently they cannot afford to lose sales in six big states by having even one movie rejected or cut to pieces. The six state censor boards have the power by law to ruin the big movie companies.

15

PRIVATE LIFE OF THE MOVIE

Art has no morality but the intangible code of beauty. To the censor, morality—his morality—is art. Caught between the fearful producer and the censor, no director has a chance to make a movie for men and women.

Although they are merely petty politicians, it is extraordinary how well the censors have kept their activities and their personalities secret. They refuse to admit their work. They will not submit to interviews. Go to any movie executive and ask him about the state censors. Those who have met the censors refuse to talk about them. They are afraid, actually afraid, of these people. Each movie company has a corps of diplomats, delegated to work and soothe these state censors. These men would not discuss the work of the censors. "We might get in trouble." A $2,500 a year politician has the power to humiliate and cow a $100,000 executive. It's a good show.

We list in this chapter a few of the important cuts made in 1928-29, and give you brief glimpses of the type of men and women in charge of the state censorship boards.

16

"LOVE." Greta Garbo and John Gilbert playing the lovers in a dramatization of Anna Karenina. Note: They had to be married before they could love in Pennsylvania.

THE SAINTS AT WORK

THE APOSTLES OF VIRGINIA

It is only fair to the august body of Virginians to admit that they are the most lenient of the six state boards.

In "A Woman of Affairs" the Virginia apostles gave this order: "Shorten to flash of five feet scene of Diana and Holderness on couch, embracing and kissing—and eliminate view of Diana's hand except after she has dropped her ring." This is an important command. This movie was taken from Michael Arlen's best seller "The Green Hat." In the novel, read in every state in the union by young and old, a girl marries a man who commits suicide on her bridal night. When asked by the coroner for some explanation, she answers: "Boy Fenwick died for purity!" The inference was that she was a damaged woman and when the bridegroom discovered it he committed suicide. After several chapters of breezy, amusing literature, the author explains that the bridegroom had syphilis and thus it was he, not his bride, who was damaged.

PRIVATE LIFE OF THE MOVIE

The Hays office decreed "The Green Hat" unfit for the great pure movie public (which had finished the book and read it the second time months since). The producer changed the name to "A Woman of Affairs," casually explaining under the title that it was taken from the Arlen novel, thus leaving the origin of the movie a deep secret. However, the node of the story, the venereal bridegroom, must not find its way into a movie plot. The "censors wouldn't allow it." The hero is made an embezzler instead of a victim of a well-represented social disease and commits suicide for "decency" rather than "purity," purity being the word the movie readers would have recognized.

Thus emasculated, "A Woman of Affairs" got through Virginia, except for the ring scene. The significance of that is explained by the fact that the heroine tells the man she has always loved, and from whom she was separated because of her presumed disgrace, that the ring represented a barrier to her honour, or words to that effect, and that when it slipped, so did she. In the following scene Greta Garbo and John Gilbert sit on a couch and a close-up of her hand shows the ring falling to the floor. Now "A Woman of Affairs" was no cheap movie, it was well-acted and contained as much restraint and dignity as the book; yet in Virginia a woman cannot lose her honour, or virginity, in the movies; although she may be losing it by the hour at the corner book store.

In "Moulin Rouge" they eliminated a series of scenes showing bare-legged girls "as they indecently kick." Only a movie censor could tell when a kick is indecent.

In "Homecoming" * the gentlemen of the South ordered: "Reduce to a five-foot flash a scene in which the hero 'stands with evident desire and looks towards Anna's room . . .' also reduce to a three-foot flash scene in which Anna lies in bed with cover restlessly thrown off and shows her desire for Karl by gestures and facial expressions."

"Homecoming" was a beautiful and simple German movie based on a story of two comrades separated by the war. One comrade re-

* "Homecoming" was adapted from the novel "Carl and Anna." A dramatization of it is now being played by a Theatre Guild company in New York City. Not even John S. Sumner has spoken against the play.

turns home, friendless, hungry, penniless. He believes his friend to be dead. He goes to the wife of his friend to explain this. She is almost penniless, is equally lonely. She feeds the man, lodges him. He explains her husband has been captured, probably killed, by the Russians. The two people are subsequently torn between a logical desire for each other and the memory of their mutual friend. After days of severe discipline they consummate their desire. The husband returns home, discovers the relationship, understands the circumstances, and when he sees the wife prefers his friend, leaves home and gives them his blessing. Yet it looked bad in Virginia; the evil head of desire was crushed to a three-foot flash.

For no reason that any sane man or woman could understand, the Virginia censors ordered "close-ups of bride in Pullman berth where she registers expectation" cut from "The Crowd." Now if the scene were as gross as the censor's explanation you might naturally presume that the heroine came leaping into the berth with her hair flying, a bottle of gin in one hand and a Margaret Sanger text-book in

"THE CROWD." Eleanor Boardman could comb her hair and give a superb performance in the great movie in every state but Virginia.

the other. As a matter of fact it was one of the most delicate, restrained performances ever given in a movie. Eleanor Boardman, an intelligent and capable young lady, in appearance and action, did this magnificent job. "The Crowd" was among the best movies made by an American director in 1928. Yet a fine piece of work, for once restrained, and handled by an artist, was cut because the ladies and gentlemen of the old South had been spending too much time over custard pie comedies and movie-fan-magazines to understand real artistry.

"Unwelcome Children" was rejected and thrown out of the state. The movie was not important; the comment was: "This film is a photoplay with a clearly defined well-acted plot, but it involves such delicate questions as *eugenics, birth control, and abortion, contraceptives and the like.* It is the unanimous opinion of the members of this division that these questions, whatever their merit, *are not fit material for exploitation on the motion picture screen.* . . . The story embodies a most repulsive scene, the rape of a young woman social

21

worker by an imbecile whom she has befriended. On this hideous crime the plot hinges; to eliminate it would destroy the continuity of the story and make it senseless. It requires no liberal interpretation of the censorship law to find 'Unwelcome Children' offending, not only on account of its inhuman features but also through its obscenity and indecency. Possibly, also, it might incite some classes to crime."

We have given you only a few deletions out of over six thousand dictated by the Virginia censors in one year. Most of these deletions were "sex" deletions, such things as indecent kicking and the like. Important or not, the whole thing was expensive to the tax-payers, the theatre owners, and absolutely useless. No movie scene actually proving the absurd theory that a man and woman under certain conditions might enjoy sexual intercourse out of wedlock was passed by the board. Against this rigid moral standard we can prove that *Scribner's Magazine* is not barred from the newsstands in Virginia, and that this highly respectable magazine contained information and dialogue infinitely more suggestive than the dropping of a ring from the hand of Greta Garbo in "A Woman of Affairs."

In the August, 1929 issue of *Scribner's,* Ernest Hemingway's "A Farewell to Arms" carried the following dialogue:

" 'Come on. We'll both get drunk and be cheerful. Then we'll get the ashes dragged. Then we'll feel fine.' " Again: " 'He's very tired and overworked,' he said. 'He thinks too he has syphilis. I don't believe it but he may have. He's treating himself for it.' "

Now it is not our purpose to brand *Scribner's* as a pornographic sheet, but as one of the most highly regarded and respectable magazines in America. The dialogue fits the subject undertaken by Hemingway, and Virginia so far has raised no protest.

Indignant note:

I—The movies were restrained by the Hays Office from using a syphilitic subject even for a moment in "A Woman of Affairs."

II—The Virginia censors would not allow a scene showing a woman letting a ring drop from her finger in this purified movie.

III—*Scribner's* prints dialogue suggesting illicit love and venereal disease, and is *read openly in Virginia.*

The Virginia board of censors makes no pretence of working for the public good. It admits that it is engaged in a profitable, if unusual business. In its report to the governor at the end of 1928 it started off with the amazing statement: "Business steadily increases. Never before in the history of censorship has the volume of business been so great. The total reelage inspected was 6230 as against 5944 in the preceding year. The total receipts for 1927-28 were $27,624.75. The nearest approach to this came in 1924-5 when the excess of receipts over expenses cleared a total of $4,838.13."

We can thus conclude that the cutting of "A Woman of Affairs" in order to avoid showing the citizens a scene intimating that men and women love out of wedlock, and the annihilation of the beautiful German "Homecoming" were merely business matters, committed in order to make a good report for the governor. Under the title "Pruning Knife Busy" the board boasts of the proud fact that it cut more movies than ever before. "Never before in Virginia," cries the board, "have there been so many deletions, either of scenes or subtitles. This means that the pictures which did offend, in many cases were objectionable or offensive in several particulars. Some were subjected to six or eight cuts, others to even more."

The Board very courteously refuses to take all the credit for this enviable record of its banner business year. It devotes a paragraph to acknowledging its volunteer help. "The members of this division again take the occasion to express their sense of obligation to the corps of volunteer inspectors assisting them in the various cities and towns of the state. These unselfish assistants who work without compensation and often at great inconvenience to themselves, never fail to respond to an emergency call. Furthermore, they exercise constant vigilance in their efforts to prevent the exhibition of unlicensed pictures, and to see that deleted films displayed outside of Richmond have been 'cut' in accordance with instructions by this department."

PRIVATE LIFE OF THE MOVIE

As the Virginia board makes no effort to disguise the fact that it is primarily out for business, not purity, no matter what the motivation of its corps of unselfish assistants, it is not surprising to find the members of the board a fairly shrewd group of politicians. The Chairman of the Board, Evan R. Chesterman, has been chairman ever since the creation of his board in 1922. He is the son of a former editor of the *Richmond Dispatch,* and is a graduate of Richmond College. He tried his hand at law, but gave it up after six months.

He has written several books for boys, and is spoken of in Richmond as a very kind and pleasant man. He is practically an invalid and spends much of his time in a wheel chair. He is 59 years old.

The second member of the board is Mrs. Emma Speed Sampson. She is supposed to be a descendant of John Keats, but for the sake of literature we haven't investigated the rumour. She also does movie reviews for the *Richmond Dispatch.*

The third member of the board is Richard

THE SAINTS AT WORK

Moncure, one time State Senator, and politician of many years service.

Thus, so far as art and morality in the movies are concerned, the citizens of Virginia are served by a semi-politician, a descendant of Keats, and an out-and-out politician. It is commendable that this amiable group has made no attempt either in its work or its history to clothe its actions in sanctity, but has frankly admitted that as political job-holders it is necessary for them to make a good showing and increase their production, even though at times it is necessary to ruin the work of a dozen acknowledged artists. Yet, somehow, we seem to see the loose-limbed figure of the gaunt, tired author of the Declaration of Independence stalking the hillside of Monticello, looking over the winding boundaries of the school he built, and wondering whether, after all, it was worth it.

THE OHIO SAINTS

The movie censors of Ohio take their work seriously. Unlike the amiable Virginians, they

27

do not consider themselves merely public servants—from their work we can understand that they are determined to crush the evil spirit of unholy love even though they are forced to destroy a thousand expensive reels of film in doing it. In Ohio even a gesture may be interpreted as indecent, and as for any amorous action—well, the producers might as well not try to get them in Ohio. The great movie public of Ohio is not to be denied its simple faith in the stork.

No movie of any importance was passed by the ladies and gentlemen of Ohio without some unholy gesture being snatched from it, with the exceptions of the story of Christ, "The King of Kings," and Charlie Chaplin's "The Circus." Everything else of importance was cut some way or another. We have selected samples of the work done to a few important and expensive productions.

From "The Barker," a movie taken from a successful and uncensored stage play, they ordered: "Cut out scenes showing man removing woman's clothing from his berth, and eliminate scene of boy and girl in orchard where

"Street of Sin." The look that was sent out of Ohio.

girl is shown lying on ground." The girl in question marries the boy at the conclusion of this drama of carnival life, and in the wayward scene she did nothing but lie on the ground, but it aroused too many suspicions for the Ohioians to give it their blessing.

From "Sins of the Fathers" they ordered cut a scene showing Ruth Chatterton in her underwear. They had a peculiar reaction to a very amusing and harmless scene in "The Magnificent Flirt." A splendid movie, turned out by a brilliant young Frenchman and a well-known playwright, it contained a scene wherein a Parisian roué watches a young lady take her morning exercise in a neighbouring apartment. His nephew comes into the room, so he points out the show to him. The boy sees an airplane stunting and believes it the cause of his uncle's entertainment. There is some very amusing dialogue until the old man observes his nephew's error and proceeds to chide him for it. "I show you a beautiful young woman," he explains "and you look at an airplane—you pervert!"

The Ohio board said: "Strike out the word 'pervert.'" Now either the word itself frightened the board, or from seeing too many movies they read into the caption a very sinister and difficult meaning, because to a normal man or woman it was nothing but a very amusing wise-crack. The Ohio board is steeped in fear of this kind. It ordered a long scene cut from "Street of Sin" because "of expression on man's face as he looks at Salvation Army girl." The actor was Emil Jannings and it is indeed complimentary even to him for the board to suggest that the mere memory of the look on his face would turn tender Ohioians into raving predatory beasts, and cause them to rush out of the movie theatres with lust dripping from their eyes. Possibly Jannings was thinking of the beer back home, or had eaten too much breakfast, but in Ohio it was shameful, that look.

Day in and day out the Ohio board toils and labours in this worthy fashion. From "Drums of Love," a very lovely D. W. Griffith production, they ordered: "Cut scenes showing hero in tight trousers bowing and standing at top of stairway. Cut view of him walking (still in tight trousers)." As the board never explains,

30

we are forced to conclude that either they feared a recurrence of the tight trouser fashion in men's wear in Ohio or else they are possessed of esoteric facts convincing them that a man in tight trousers is a menace to a clean community.

The board cut "The Man Who Laughs" almost to pieces. This assault becomes even more fantastic when you consider that Victor Hugo's book, from which it was taken, has been read in Christian communities for the last fifty years. The movie did full justice to the book. It was a serious, restrained, magnificent job, directed by a brilliant German, Paul Leni. The villainess of the story, Josiana, one of the most famous characters in fiction, is a sadistic seventeenth century Duchess. The part was taken by Baclanova, a Russian actress who was given unanimous praise all over the country when she first appeared with the Moscow Art Players several years ago. Almost every one of her scenes was cut. These are a few of the eliminations demanded by the Ohio board from this very superior movie:

"All scenes of men looking through key-hole."

"Scene of Duchess with leg on chair."

"Duchess at Fair where man pulls dress off shoulder."

"All seductive scenes between Duchess and Jester, *that is,* all scenes where Duchess and Jester appear together."

The censors in Ohio are simple people. To them a leg is a leg, a woman is a woman, and a look at a leg has only one meaning and conclusion. They might well be proud that they have left the intangible and difficult definitions of art and life to more complex people. They themselves are not interested. Be it written by a bell-hop or created by the hand of an acknowledged artist, any scene between a man or woman becomes dubious the minute they come within thirty-five feet of each other. And Ohio doesn't stand for it. The tax-payers of that great Middle-Western state, housing the Cincinnati and the Cleveland Symphony and the home-town of Warren G. Harding, should be proud of their guardians.

"Sins of the Fathers." The underwear wasn't magazine advertising. It couldn't go in Ohio.

THE SAINTS AT WORK

The censorship set-up in Ohio is practically the same as that of New York State.

The board has been put in charge of the Department of Education. Two civil service employees, at $200 a month, work under the supervision of the Ohio Director of Education. Their terms of office are dependent upon "good behaviour"; although, of course, if anybody has temptation and vice knocking at his door, a movie censor must be hard beset. In 1929, $23,000 were given these two faithful servants for office expenses.

There is also an advisory board of two men and a lady appointed by the governor. They receive no money—merely "expenses." According to the attorney-general this board functions only when the Department of Education needs help—which, in Ohio, must be infrequent.

John Leroy Clifton, the head man of the Ohio board, is a teacher and a politician. He was born in 1881 in Etna, Ohio. He taught in rural schools and attended Ohio University during his spare time.

In 1916 he was made an assistant professor

33

at Ohio State University, and appointed professor in 1917. In 1927 he was given leave of absence by the university to accept the appointment of State Superintendent of Public Instruction and Director of Education for Ohio. That makes him head of the present censor board, one of his minor duties.

He is a large, black-haired round-faced professor, and an enthusiastic ball fan. He wrote his doctor's thesis on the subject "The small secondary school in Ohio."

It is this man who accepts the reports of his life-term $200-a-month assistants; a professor who agrees that Hugo is salacious literature and that tight pants are an evil insignia to a virtuous community.

THE SAINTS OF MARYLAND

The movies receive two or three purifying processes before they ever reach the eyes of the state boards. Yet these gentlemen are still whimsical and superior enough in their moral judgments to find something wrong in most of the films they review. Maryland censors reviewed nine thousand movies last year, and cut something out of five hundred.

There is a charming humour about the habits of these boards. Certainly they cannot be accused of standardization of purity. A thumb against a nose is a felony in Kansas, and an amusing gesture in Maryland. But the Maryland brethren have decreed that a kiss on the neck is worth three or four hundred any-where else; we find over one hundred com-mands during six months last year to "elimi-nate scene where Oswald kisses Esther on neck." The ordinary man is not equipped to understand the insidious evil suggestion con-tained in a lusty neck osculation, and we have Maryland to thank for this subtle definition of erotic behaviour. As might be expected in the State of Ritchie, whiskey and flasks that never see the light of day in Kansas have no trouble from the hands of the Marylanders.

Among other things, Maryland concurred with Virginia on the ring-from-finger episode in "A Woman of Affairs," and Arlen's heroine goes into the free state with no scores against her.

Suggestions of illegitimacy were eliminated from "Betrayal," the Emil Jannings movie. This minor elimination merely ruined the entire plot of the story, which had not one indecent gesture in it.

In "Interference" the individuality of the censor again shows its colouring; the Maryland chairman being a druggist, he demanded the elimination of "scene showing Ackfold putting poison in glass," and "scene showing Deborah drinking poisoned liquor," as well as "all scenes showing labels marked 'poison' or 'prussic acid.'"

"Interference" was the first important talkie made in America. Taken from the successful stage play of the same name, the movie contained an excellent cast, good direction, and in every way was a serious and dignified artistic effort. As the plot of the story revolves around a poison murder, the elimination of the above scenes merely ruined the story and point of "Interference." This piece of property cost well over $100,000, it was seen in practically every other state in the Union, with its poison labels intact, yet because Providence chose a druggist

36

to enforce its higher dictates in the land of the *Baltimore Sun* and Johns Hopkins University, the most important scenes in the movie were dropped into Chesapeake Bay.

The decision of the board regarding two movies offers a clear picture of the intellectual height, the artistic judgment, and the general standards of the Maryland censor board. A movie called "Fighting the White Slave Traffic" was passed after a great many title deletions. From reading these one may get a general idea of the kind of drama it was: "Along the streets walk scarlet women once innocent who were forced into a life of shame by the subtle wiles and crafty methods of the white slaver; in the cabarets of Tia Juana are many girls of every nationality who were lured into its vice-ridden places by fake vaudeville contracts; etc., etc." All point out the dangers besetting the innocent flowers of vaudeville every time they sign a dotted line. Obviously this movie, made by an independent company with no rank or standing in the business, is one of those old-timers shown in stale dowdy movie houses on the West Side "For Women Only"

37

and then moved over to the East Side and advertised "For Men Only." The point is, with a few deletions, the Maryland board passed this meretricious bit of sanctimonious pornography.

At the same time the board ordered two scenes cut from "Sunrise"; "scene of woman and man reclining," and "scene of woman wriggling and dancing and man embracing her." Now if you were to take the brethren at their word the description "woman wriggling and dancing and man embracing her" would naturally cause you to visualize a couple of vaudeville "little Evas" trying to shimmy their way out of a Tia Juana bordello. Again, the mere deletion of two scenes does not seem such a fearful elimination.

However, "Sunrise" is a movie worth fighting for. The man or woman who could look upon this movie and find even one scene dirty or suggestive is a man or woman who has been titillated too many times by drama such as "Fighting the White Slave Traffic." The critic who could pass "The White Slave Traffic" and then cut "Sunrise" is the type of man

38

who could spend eight hours looking at two-
for-a-nickel art magazines and then issue an
order to burn a Raphael nude. He could read
Elinor Glynn all night and then demand that
Theodore Dreiser be put in solitary confine-
ment. In other words, he is a man who has
sought trash and suggestion in such low planes
that he is no more fit to judge art, drama, literature or everyday ethics than the editor of a
bankrupt tabloid newspaper.

"Sunrise" was directed by Murnau, the Aus-
trian who probably has been more responsible
for putting the movie in its place and establish-
ing it as an artistic medium worthy of respect
than any other director in the world. The scene
cut out in Maryland was brilliant and effective.
It is not so much that this cut hurt a great
movie, as that a really artistic piece of work,
conceived and directed by an artist of note, was
damaged by a group of people who had been
spending eight hours a day in a stuffy projection room seeing mile after mile of comedies,
and dull enervating Hollywood romances, until their brains were dulled into pronouncing
it unfit for the citizens of Maryland.

PRIVATE LIFE OF THE MOVIE

In 1916 the General Assembly of Maryland enacted a law creating a State Board of movie censors, stating that it "shall consist of three residents and citizens of the State of Maryland, one of whom shall be a member of the political party polling the second highest vote at the election prior to their appointment. . . . For the examination of each 1,000 feet of motion picture film the Board shall receive in advance a fee of $1.00. The salaries of each member of the board shall be $2,400 per annum for each member."

In 1920 the board reported that it had reviewed 5,335 films and censored 1,192. It collected $41,153.69 for this work, of which $12,544.04 went for wages and salaries.

Eight years later, the board, under the same chairman, reported that it had examined 9,377 films and censored 485. It collected $38,-165.57 of which $22,137.67 went for wages.

It is interesting to note that during the past few years many volunteers have come forward to support the board. In its annual report the board states that it was "greatly indebted to the Women's Civic League for its co-operation

40

"Sunrise." The brilliant and effective scene cut in Maryland.

in furnishing an inspector to work under the direction of the board, for the board, for the greater part of the year . . . Paid inspection has shown immediate results in better enforcement of the law. The Board has been obliged to rely on volunteers in the Counties, and as this is not entirely satisfactory a request for two additional inspectors at salaries of $900 each has been submitted to the legislature."

And so we find that the three politically appointed guardians of the pure have not been able to satisfactorily cover fifty-four miles of film a week and have called upon volunteer saviours in "the counties." The citizens of Maryland have had their movies cut and hacked by the type of man or woman who, either for the sheer love of purity, or $900 a year, would sit and gaze upon reel after reel of Hollywood film.

As a chart for sailing the boundless seas of evil, the board has postulated its code of morals. Any movie violating these was censored.

"Suggestive comedy, stories built on illicit love, over-passionate love scenes, disrespect of

41

the law and condonation of crime by officers of the law, men and women living together in adultery and without marriage, drinking and gambling made attractive, prolonged success to criminals, profanity in titles, maternity scenes, stories and incidents showing disrepect of any religion, advocacy of the doctrine of free love, and titles calculated to stir up racial hatred and antagonistic relations between labour and capital."

Which leaves the story of Cinderella (without the ball), Little Red Riding Hood (without the wolf), and the Life of George Washington (without the rum), as about the only dramatic material the movies can employ in Maryland.

The chairman of the board rates a better education than any other board chairman. Dr. George Heller has been entrusted for nine years with this job. It is this man, with his worldly experience, who has been able to determine that a kiss on the neck is loaded with dynamite, that a ring dropped from the finger is liable to increase the birth rate, and that pictures of poison labels might decrease the divorce rate and help the undertaking business.

Allow us to present Dr. George Heller, druggist, jurist, politician, and chairman of the Maryland board of movie censors since 1920. Fifty-five years old, he has lived in and about Baltimore all his life; he now lives half a square from the house in which he was born. He was graduated from city schools, and entered the City College. Tiring of text-books and dull lectures, he left school to go to work in order that he might fit himself for his life's calling. He first got a job in a brush factory tying hair on brushes. He left this interesting employment at the end of the first day and turned to the jewellery business. This employment proved to be much more varied and worldly in that the jeweller maintained a printing shop (and printers are notoriously worldly fellows). The young crusader learned the printing trade. He gave this up one day when he carelessly forgot to pull his hand from the jaws of the press.

About this time Dr. Heller's father decided

that his son had the artistic eye, and determined he should become a clothing designer. His son followed the parental judgment and worked at this business for a year. It still wasn't the answer. Somewhere, somehow there was a great good to be done in the world, and Heller had not yet discovered it. After a year designing clothes he decided to become a druggist. Starting as a drug clerk, he studied at nights and was graduated from the Maryland College of Pharmacy in 1895. Yet even this was not the answer. The future board chairman had not yet wrested the information from the world necessary to pry into the dark corners of man's mind and determine those depths which should be guarded and protected from evil. He decided to become a doctor, and was graduated two years later from the Maryland University. He then began the practice of medicine, and bought a drugstore which he still runs, such time as he is not immersed in movie-censoring.

What time he has left after being a doctor, censor, and druggist, Dr. Heller devotes to politics. He has run for Congress, and he is a

44

Democrat and a Wet. He is married, the father of three children, and is a Lutheran.

Happy the people of Maryland. Not a monk, not a cloistered man, but a hair-tyer, jeweler, printer, clothing designer, druggist, doctor, politician, is responsible for the character of over $100,000,000 worth of movies that enter the State of Maryland each year. He should go down in history as one of the most versatile and important men ever connected with American art.

THE SAINTS OF KANSAS

The guardians of the pure in Kansas are just about as talented as you would expect them to be. Kansas does show a logical contrast with Virginia in that in no instance was a movie allowed to show prolonged drinking scenes, and all titles containing the dread word "whiskey" were promptly cast away, as well as all scenes showing flasks or bottles that might indicate that outside the sober borders of Kansas a debauched citizenry engaged in drinking. You may have played bridge for sixteen hours straight, or counted box cars until you were blind, or read "Peter Rabbit" to your nephew until you were dithering, but next to keeping score for a billiard tournament you could not imagine a more enervating task than prying into the actions of the Kansas state board of motion picture censors.

While it religiously strikes down any attempts at luring the dry Kansans to crave drink or the sight of an exposed female leg, the Kansas board betrays several interesting idiosyncracies all its own. In "Captain Swagger," "Sadie Thompson," "Cloud Dodgers" and "Marked Money," "Women They Talk About" and almost a hundred other movies— said the Kansas censors: "Strike out scene showing character thumbing nose."

In "Manhattan Cocktail" they ordered: "A reduction of struggle between lovers, leaving but one scene on couch." In Kansas love is not immoral by commitment; but by repetition.

In "Our Dancing Daughters" they ordered the following deletions: "Cut out scenes of Ben kissing Diana, and following scene showing them on ground in reclining position. Also

46

eliminate close view of dancers on yacht and title: 'Why are you working? Haven't you any pretty daughters—doll 'em up, a rich man wants his money's worth.' "

Now that last title, ordered out, was spoken by a drunken young married woman who has obtained a husband by tricking him into thinking her a home-loving innocent child. She subsequently falls down the stairs and breaks her neck. She is speaking to a group of scrubwomen at the foot of the stairs. For some mysterious reason her statement, logical with her character, jarred the sensibilities of the Kansans. It is hard to understand just what is particularly evil in it, but then, after all, this is Kansas.

The boys and girls had a good time with "Dry Martini," a gay and pleasing if light movie, taken from a book by that name not, so far as the records show, barred from the state of Kansas. The following deletions were ordered from this corrupting and filthy piece of celluloid:

"Eliminate title: 'With the coming of the

47

Great American Thirst in 1919, a second expeditionary force set sail for Paris.' "

"Eliminate title: 'Joseph, I'm about to become a father.' " (The man's grown daughter is coming to visit him.)

"Eliminate title: 'Prepare the guest room for my daughter as soon as it is vacant.' " (A woman has been staying therein.)

"Eliminate title: 'And this gentleman is not, I trust, a son who has escaped my memory.' "

"Eliminate close view of hairpin."

And so it goes in Kansas. Day in and day out the men and women with the purity of a state at stake toil and labour and purify the wicked products of a drunken East and an erotic West. Some future historian might thank us for going on and on to definitely explain the morals of Kansas by pointing out that whiskey, thumbing of noses, legs, and kisses, constitute an ominous threat against the fragile morality of grain growers, but we fear for our readers' and publisher's minds if we go on. Let us glance for a moment and step into a Kansas board meeting and see just what sort of people they are, these nose-thumbing haters.

"Our Dancing Daughters." Cut in Kansas.

THE SAINTS AT WORK

You could almost picture the Chairman of the Kansas board of movie censors without using her portrait. She is a real Kansan, and has never lived out of her state. She was born in Crawford county, and lived there all her life before she went to Kansas City to take up her greatest work.

Miss Emma Viets, of Girard, Kansas. Fifty or more. Former owner of the movie theatre of Girard, Kansas, where she could observe the reactions of the coal miners and foreigners who predominated in her home town. In 1919 she sold the theatre and moved to Kansas City, having been appointed a member of the censor board. In 1922 she was named chairman of the board, and will continue as such until 1932. Two other women help her, but Miss Viets, by experience and knowledge, is the real dictator of the board.

She is willing to talk about her work. "It is necessary to cut many movies," says Miss Viets.

"It is incredible how much that is questionable can be insinuated into an otherwise innocent and interesting picture. Needlessly insinuated, for *in most places it destroys the*

49

continuity of the story and has no bearing on the plot.

"Sometimes something intangible will give a twist to a picture that brings it close to the borderline of rejection. Such things as the ending of the beautiful picture "Sorrell and Son" for instance. I advised cutting out the ending where the son administers the overdose of poison to his father.

"From a humanitarian point of view it may have been all right. But it was ethically wrong. Physicians felt uncomfortable about it. (She gave no instance of a physician objecting). It opened up new vistas of thought and speculation. *The film was long anyway and could stand cutting.* It now ends where the father sinks down at the garden gate among his roses, his work of fathering finished. It is more artistic, deeper in pathos, less shocking in many minds.

"It is our job to help the moving picture fulfill its avowed purpose—to amuse the public in a clean wholesome way.

"I often go to the motion pictures in the evening," concludes Miss Viets, rocking quietly in her modest room in the Grand Hotel. "For three reasons: I like amusement, I like to find the public's opinion of amusement, and I wish to see if the censorship is observed."

It is pleasing to note that Miss Viets artistic position has not gone unrewarded. She holds the title of Right Worthy Associate Grand Matron of the Eastern Star of the World. This office expires in 1931, and even if she does not continue as chairman of the censor board she expects to get raised to the next office of this Masonic order, Most Worthy Grand Matron, which is the highest that can be given.

A gentle lady who has been in the movie business, who has always lived in Kansas, and who, after seeing 30,000 feet of film a day, goes to the movies at night for amusement! Surely Kansas is fortunate in its choice for a censor. Not only does Miss Viets censor "that which is questionable" but she exercises her undisputed ability to correct "the continuity of the story." Some states might object to allowing a lady to change the plot of a story written by a reputable English novelist, but we feel sure Kansas would not be included in that society. Certainly, a Crawford Countian should be more capable of arranging art and drama for her fellow-citizens than an Oxford graduate. Of all the state censors, Miss Viets seems peculiarly fitted to give her tax-payers what they want, and what they deserve.

THE SAINTS OF PENNSYLVANIA

Pennsylvania has the distinction at the present time of supporting the most arbitrary and severe board of censors known to the history of that state. Not since the Quakers drove Penn's governors out of the city of brotherly love has a body of people so severely protected the public morals. No censor board in the country can compete with the Pennsylvanians. Movies that go untouched in every other state in the union are hacked and retitled in Pennsylvania; movies that are slightly touched by the other boards are cut to pieces, resulting in enormous expense for movie companies and inanity for the public. No political power or pressure from the Hays office has served to break down the severity of this state board.

Each board has betrayed its own peculiar

52

Miss Emma Viets. "The film was long and needed cutting."

dislikes in its censoring. Kansas suppresses nose-thumbing; Maryland, neck-kissing; Virginia, untoward remarks. Pennsylvania rises above them all in ingenuity. Not only does this board cut at will, but they create their own art, and no man could accuse them of being non-constructive critics.

The following examples give ample proof of the fertile, creative spirit of the Pennsylvania board.

They ordered these changes in "The Barker."

For title: "I've got a quart of white mule and a pair of purple bloomers I've been saving for a night like this," substitute: "I've got a quart of bootleg gin I've been saving for a night like this."

For: "Ever since that night in the peach orchard I feel that we belong to each other," substitute: "Right at the first time I saw you I knew that I was not going to be able to help loving you."

For: "It made a bum out of me and now it's sent my boy to hell," substitute: "It's wrecked my life and now it's sent my boy to hell."

53

For: "We'd better put him to bed," substitute: "If Nifty finds him like this there'll be trouble."

"Cut scene of girl helping friend undress."

One of the authors of "The Barker" is a college professor. The play, a successful New York production, was a realistic portrayal of carnival life, the love interest being carried by an innocent youngster and a carnival "gal" who in the end marry, and make good. The movie followed the play with exceptional success. It was a talkie and very well done. If you glance back at the substitutions you can see that:

I—No substitution changed the essence of the story.

II—None of the created titles helped either the drama or the grammar.

However, the creative itch constantly urges the Pennsylvania board.

From "Oh, Kay" they ordered the title: "We'll make this place into a real fairyland" changed to: "We'll make this place a beauty bower." Lavender into old lace.

For "Fazil" they ordered: "Insert newspaper notice of marriage before showing bedroom scene."

From the "Red Dance" they ordered the caption: "I like them fatter, especially in winter" shortened to a modest: "I like them fatter."

From "Romance of the Underworld" they ordered: "If you need dough there's a real live out-of-town granpa—go to work on him" changed to: "If you can't be more sociable, there's a real live out-of-town Granpa. Maybe you'll find him more agreeable."

From "Awakening" they ordered the caption: "Von Hagen can take any woman—if he wants her he'll take her" changed to: "Von Hagen can win any woman—if he wants to he can win her." They also ordered cut a scene in which the heroine registers fear after being kissed by the hero.

From "Lights of New York" they changed title reading: "The Hawk's girl for more years than she cared to admit," to: "The Hawk's promised wife, backed him in her small way financially and loved him in her big-hearted way." From the standpoint of creative art, this change was a real achievement.

From "Beau Broadway" they ordered a puzzling elimination. They changed the caption: "He's the best-known fight promoter, gambler and race track man in America" so that the word 'gambler' was deleted. The only inference is that the Pennsylvanians very courteously declined to darken the names of its fight promoters and racing men.

From "Our Dancing Daughters" they ordered the caption: "Before I met you things happened. Were they of our crowd?" changed to: "Before I met you I was madly infatuated with a boy. Was he of our crowd?"

They also cut the scene under a tree where the hero embraces the heroine, from the point where they first embrace each other to where they are shown sitting again.

From "Sins of the Fathers" the caption: "He's so dumb we don't have to be careful" was changed to: "He's so dumb we can get away with anything." Another creative achievement.

From "Win that Girl" they cut scene of

"Docks of New York." Humor and sex can not meet in Pennsylvania. One of the scenes cut.

matches set up (presumably) to represent man and woman in embrace, wherein the burning matches bend, contort, etc. You can't play with fire in Pennsylvania.

From "Docks of New York" they cut a scene in which a stevedore is leaving a woman's bedroom. He counts out some money for her, glances at her sleeping form, and then, after deliberating, counts out an extra fee.

This eliminated scene did not mar this very excellent movie, but it aroused speculation. A stevedore rescues a streetwalker who has attempted suicide. In a drunken brawl he marries her. In the morning he sobers up, counts out a usual fee for her and leaves. After he goes she gets in trouble. He leaves his ship, comes back to her. It was a picture full of beautiful photography, directed by Von Sternberg. The elimination of the bedroom scene in no way destroyed the grim reality, the sordid background of the story. The scene was only one of many grim incidents. However, it was funny, and that is the only reason the censors could have had for choosing to eliminate it,

57

otherwise they would have rejected the entire movie.

From "Freedom of the Press" they cut note reading: "You and your dirty sheet lay off. Remember the Canton, Ohio case and the murder of Dan Mellet." It is impossible to understand the reason for this cut. Every paper in the country demanded the apprehension of the murderers of Mellet, the Canton, Ohio editor who fought the underworld so savagely it exterminated him. You could not give undue publicity to the memory of such a man. Any newspaper reader in any city in the country read something of the case. Yet it could not be mentioned in a movie in the state of Pennsylvania, in the cities of Philadelphia, Pittsburgh, et al. But try to understand any of these cuts.

They ordered a caption in "Her Cardboard Lover" reading: "I told her you were sick in bed with a nurse and she said that was when you needed her most" changed to read: "I told her you were sick in bed and she said that was when you needed her most."

In "Beware of Bachelors" they found the caption: "Do you think this bed is big enough for two?" changed to read: "Another pillow?" which, one must admit, is more succinct, better craftsmanship.

These cuts have been selected at random from the thousands ordered during 1928. Hardly a movie passes through the hands of the board without some alteration. In order to give you some idea of the severity of their treatment we shall give you the entire eliminations demanded by the board in two excellent and popular movies:

"The Racket" and "The Patriot."

The following cuts were ordered from "The Racket."

"Cut views of Scarzi pulling man's coat open and pointing to gun strapped on him and the title 'If Spike tries to stop you——'"

"All views of gangsters shooting at police; all views of men shooting from car."

"Title reading 'Habeas Corpus' for the release of Nicholas Scarzi—signed by the Judge!" changed to delete the words: "Signed by the Judge."

"All views of clergymen at crook's funeral service."

"For caption 'I'm State's Attorney Welch' substitute: 'I'm Attorney Welch.'"

"Scene where Scarzi actually shoots policeman."

"For caption 'I'm sick of the law' substitute: 'I'm sick of you flim-flamming the law.'" (The grammar is Pennsylvania.)

"The Racket" was written by a Chicago newspaper man and enjoyed a successful run on the New York stage. It was one of the best plays of the season. In cold effective dialogue it told the story of an honest police captain in Chicago struggling to maintain his self-respect against the enormous corrupt machinery of his city and state. Since that play and movie at least a dozen books have been published incorporating the names of state's attorney Crowe, Mayor Thompson and other prominent members of the Chicago machine. The movie rated as one of the best of the year. No scene could have more effectively given you the spirit of the modern gangster's inhuman ruthlessness than the one in which Scarzi shoots a young and honest policeman in the back. Yet this scene was cut in Philadelphia, as well as any reference to corrupt officials, although Chicago politicians have become cartoon stencils for magazines and newspapers. By eliminating them Pennsylvania could not help to suppress the news of Chicago's corruption. After all, Philadelphia is not yet a desert island. Obviously, the untoward cuts made in this unusually good movie were for the censors' own satisfaction and moral approvals. They helped neither Chicago, the movies, nor the public. They must have afforded the censors some satisfaction or their work was futile.

The record of the eliminations made by the Pennsylvania board of movie censors from "The Patriot" may sound like gibberish unless you clearly recall the movie. Many people claim this is the most artistic and polished movie ever made. It is hard to think of a better one. It was taken from a play by Alfred Neuman, the distinguished German playwright. The cast was beyond reproach—it was indubitably Emil Janning's best performance in this country. Ernst Lubitsch, another German of known merit, directed him. As he, years ago, discovered the fatherly Jannings working as a strong man in a strolling troup and took him to Max Reinhardt, from whence be became one of the most popular actors in Germany, it is not difficult to see how the combination of a strong play, and the comradeship of a great actor and a skilful playwright, produced the best movie of the year. It was dignified, dramatic —above all, adult entertainment. But see what the Pennsylvania board did to "The Patriot."

"In sequence where Csar while listening to Phalen's story turns suddenly and runs through many rooms to Laphoukhina (his mistress) allow only one flash where he turns from Phalen and one flash showing him immediately at door of Laphoukhina's room."

Stopping here to interpret, this ranks as one of the most contemptible things ever done by a group of moralists. If you remember the scene, you will recall that the mad Csar is having an epilectic rage when Phalen enters the room, and in order to soothe him, Phalen whispers a presumably erotic story in his ear. At the conclusion the Csar wheels, a look of stupid cunning on his imbecilic face and races through corridor after corridor, leaving you bewildered as to what has motivated that childlike brain, until he suddenly brings up sharp before a great door—and enters his mistress' bedroom. It is a real Rabelaisian scene, good for a bellylaugh in any civilized audience. The machinations of that diseased brain, the pathetic simplicity, the dangerous madness—all are incorporated in that one swift, hilarious moment, yet Pennsylvania would not *let you see him running through the corridor!*

You may see a madman, but you may not laugh; you may fornicate, but you may not run to it, in Pennsylvania.

There are three more paragraphs of eliminations demanded by the board, all of them being scenes between the Csar and Phalen's mistress, or between Phalen and his mistress. Now these scenes were not inserted for the sake of the semi-eroticism they contain, as a thousand movies contain, and are allowed to pass into Pennsylvania by the board, but they served to show the limits to which Phalen would go for the sake of his country, for the sake of doing away with his friend the Csar. No child could have misunderstood the sacrifice, the intensity and the dignity portrayed in every scene in "The Patriot." If it was a suggestive movie, then no celluloid would ever unwind in Pennsylvania. But the very earnestness, the very reality of the shadowy figures in this movie worried the censors—so they cut and cut—and ruined some of the greatest scenes. They emasculated a piece of art acknowledged as such by a hundred civilized commentators. They refused scenes to their tax-payers witnessed by citizens of every other state in the union. And the eliminations demanded from this superb work are typical of the slashes made in movies in Pennsylvania. They accept no standards created by art, literature, drama, or even other censor boards. They work with a fury and an inconsistency that offer no clue as to what cause they purport to serve.

The members of the Pennsylvania State Board are as mysterious as their code of morals. The law giving them their existence was passed in 1911. According to the statute: "The Pennsylvania State Board of Censors shall consist of three residents and citizens of Pennsylvania, two males and one female. . . . The chairman shall receive a salary of $4,800 per annum, and the vice-chairman and the secretary shall each receive $4,500 per annum."

Despite the attempts of three reporters, the members of the board refused to discuss their work or their life. The present chairman of the board, Harry L. Knapp has been a member since 1913, and chairman since 1919.

He is dramatic editor of the *Philadelphia Inquirer,* and writes the column called "The Old Stager" which is featured in their Sunday dramatic section. He is married and lives in Norwood, Delaware county, a few miles outside the city.

Henry Starr Richardson, 444 W. Stafford Street, Germantown, has been a member of the board for about eight years, and is its secretary. He does most of the clerical work connected with the board. He is a former newspaper man.

Mrs. Mary D. Patton was appointed in August, 1928. She is the widow of State Senator Alexander Ennis Patton, and a former

State Regent and National Vice-President General of the D. A. R. Her home is in Curwensville, Clearfield county, but she maintains a winter residence in Philadelphia.

The board has its offices on the upper floor of 1222 Vine St., in the centre of the film booking district of the city.

And there they are. We do not pretend to understand their principles. Possibly the existence of a dramatic critic on the board explains the creative itch we saw in action. But no fantastic presumption would explain the principles of the board that owes its life to the political machine that knew Boise Penrose and Senator Vare.

Perhaps, they are just having fun. They may not like the movies—few dramatic critics do. But it is expensive fun for the public. The press and the citizens have winced time and time again. But so long as critic Knapp is in the saddle they will feel the curb. His record speaks for itself.

THE SAINTS AT WORK

THE SAINTS OF NEW YORK

The New York board of movie censors is the most important and the second most severe in the country. It is important in that New York City must abide by its decisions. Plays that run for years on the stage are cut to pieces when they reach movie form. You have seen what happened to "Coquette," "Rain" and the many other successful and unharmed plays when the producers tried to convert them into movies. Even though they humble themselves to the extent of going to the censors and asking them if it will be "all right" to make a movie of this or that play, after the movie comes out the censors frequently suffer conscience pangs, and decide that the citizens of Soddus Center might object, and cut the movie.

Where Pennsylvania is worried about sex, New York bites its nails over corruption. Political job-holders themselves, the New York board very logically refuses to allow any ugly

67

remarks to be passed about politicians in general.

In the movie "Me Gangster" they changed the title: "No more work for me now—I've got a politician's job" to read: "Good news— a politician's got me a real job." They cut the title: "Before I was nineteen graft and crooked politics had made pop a big power in the district." No other state touched either of these titles.

From "The Escape" they cut "Jerry Martin, sneering at the law behind the guns of his gang." From "Legion of the Condemned" they cut all scenes of roulette wheel and of coloured girls dancing, although Harlem has become a tourist's playground.

From "Ned McCobb's Daughter" they cut the title: "This place was just made to operate my booze racket from," and all scenes where man is shown labelling bottles . . . Grover Whalen announces that there are 32,000 speakeasies in the city of New York, but the moviegoers must be kept in ignorance. "Ned McCobb's Daughter" was presented without difficulties on Broadway, but two blocks away

68

it could not be shown as a movie without censorship.

In "The Body Punch" they cut scene showing a boy actually putting a brick in a prizefighter's glove.

They demanded several changes in "The Noose." This movie was taken from a successful play. Richard Barthelmess did a splendid job, the titles were lifted verbatim from the play, yet it could not pass the board, and the very people who saw the play could not see a movie-ized version. They changed the title "One of those night clubs that is helping to make Sweet Adeline the National Anthem" (certainly an innocuous remark) to read "The capitol of a mid-western state and one of its first class night clubs!" And yet the Civil War was fought seventy years ago.

They changed "When I get plenty of protection for you" to: "When I pave the road for you."

They cut "The Racket" badly.

They cut the title: "For the release of Nicholas Scarzi—signed by the Judge" so that "signed by the Judge" was eliminated. (Pennsylvania concurred in this cut necessary to protect the honour of our spotless courts.)

They cut all scenes of reporters drinking at police station.

All scenes of gangsters at crook's funeral.

Title: "Nick will have you thrown off the force, etc."

View of Scarzi offering policeman roll of bills. (Which he did not take.)

Scene of gangster deliberately shooting policeman in back.

Title: "As long as the wards are set for Tuesday night what do they care about you?"

View of state official telephoning to get gangster out of jail.

Title: "You men knew the Old Man had that kid accidentally killed last week?"

"Who do you suppose I pay for my alcohol? Who do I pay for my brewery? I'll tell on the whole damned organization, etc., etc." (This was the best speech in the play.)

Title: "Government by the professionals, of the professionals and for the professionals."

If you remember the story of "The Racket" you can piece together these cuts. The play was one of the most dramatic and realistic productions ever presented in New York City. Edward Robinson did a superb job as Scarzi, the Chicago gangster, and Louis Wolheim ably followed him in the movie. It was a straight from the shoulder drama of an honest man fighting a ponderous crooked city machine, of his humiliation and subsequent triumph over enormous, corrupt powers. The play dealt not with women, children, or flag-waving. There was not one censorable line in it—that is, not a censorable line unless you hold with the New York board that it is a crime against morality to suggest that the politicians of Chicago or any other city include unscrupulous crooks, and that gangsters of the Al Capone type pay for protection.

While the New York board of censors hits hard at suggestions of corruption it is not slow in spotting sexual inferences. From: "Gentlemen Prefer Blondes" they changed title: "Oh, my daddy" to read: "Oh, Mr. Eisman." For "You could no more hurt my girl friend's reputation than you could sink the Jewish fleet," they eliminated any reference to the Jews or their navy. For "When those birds kiss my hand I can feel it clear down to my toes" they substituted: "When they kiss my hand—oh boy."

"Gentlemen Prefer Blondes" was translated into practically every language, ran in a newspaper syndicate, was made into a comic strip, a play, and a movie. Fortunately for the movie public, the censors cut any suggestions of immorality from it, as you have seen.

New York City pays out millions for movies every year—Germany, France and England send it their best. But that best is not presentable until the board has done its work. Consider the New York daily papers, the stories of bootlegging and crime, and then think of a well-paid group of people toiling and deleting such suggestions from a movie, and wonder!

In 1927 the business of censoring movies in New York State was turned over to the department of education. The standards of the motion picture division are thus set down in the state educational law:

"No motion picture will be licensed or a

"THE RACKET." "Government of the Professionals, by the Professionals, and for the Professionals." Not allowed in the city of the "Evening Graphic." Unfit for Philadelphia. It might have influenced honest officials.

permit granted for its exhibition within the state of New York which may be classified, or any part thereof, as obscene, indecent, immoral, inhuman, sacrilegious, or which is of such a character that its exhibition would tend to corrupt morals or incite to crime."

There are over 2,000 theatres in New York State—almost a thousand in New York City. In his 1928 report, state censor James Wingate complains of the limited staff and budget allowed him by the department of education. Pointing to the great number of movie houses under his control, he says: "It can readily be seen that the Division has not a sufficient number of inspectors to do the work adequately. (There are 16 members of the division.) Such work as our limited force is able to do has resulted in materially increasing the receipts of the State and in bringing about a more general observance of the law.

"The inspection work of the Division in the smaller communities has been materially aided through the co-operation of the New York State constabulary—

"While patrolling the State these troopers

73

have inspected theatres and films and monthly reports of their visitations with reference to violations of the motion picture statute are submitted to this office."

Despite the great collection of educational experts, then, at the call of the State Department of Education, the movie—seen by 1,000,-000 people a day in New York City alone—is so unimportant that the interpretation of "indecency," "inhumanism," etc., is left to the state constabulary, usually selected for their shooting and riding ability. We could imagine their fitness to judge the merit of a Tom Mix Western, but we wonder at their ability for passing on Ibsen, Maugham or Eugene O'Neill.

Director Wingate not only finds his department inadequte for the state at large, but he admits in his report that he himself has little time for actually reviewing movies. (Even though he received an honorary degree from Union College for his masterful career in this work.)

"In as much as the reviewers are sometimes called upon to review in a single day twelve miles of film," says Director Wingate, "it is of course impossible for the Director personally to review all films submitted. His time is almost wholly taken up with administrative duties, travelling . . . and interviews with the producers and the public."

Unfortunately, New Yorkers are denied the able criticism of the degreed head of the censor board. The actual cuts are made by the three reviewers who toil from 9 to 4 each day in 42nd Street to delete scenes likely to incite crime, sacrilege, or, as you will remember, to hurt the feelings of politicians.

There is no discussion of the actual influence of the movie, of the difficult boundaries of art and morality, in the Director's report. He merely states that neither he, his board, nor the state troopers can review adequately the movies released in New York State. As they cannot even see all the movies one might well wonder how they expect their cuts to be consistent, important, or fair.

The chief censor of New York State is not of the movies. He is a teacher. He is not as proud of the fact that he is the dictator of the greatest medium of education in his state as he is of the fact that he has progressed from a Duansberg school master to his present important place in the nation's educational system.

He has the characteristics of his profession. Middle-aged, slightly pompous yet evasive, and given to long-winded and meaningless speeches. His spectacles and severe garb give him the appearance of a clergyman or a Y. M. C. A. organizer. He goes to many movie openings, often with a cleric or priest.

He was a school commissioner, 1900-12, of Schenectady county, superintendent of schools, 1912-17, and assistant in elementary education, 1917-27, when he got his censorship job.

He is a past president of the Hudson River Schoolmaster's Club, and 1917-18 was Grand Master of the New York State Grand Lodge of Odd Fellows.

If the movies were hindered only by these petty politicians, we could stop here, demand their recall and call it a day. Yet while they

76

alone are not to blame for the vapid and vulgar condition of the ordinary movie, they have the only legal power of repression in the business. They themselves are not big men and women. It is humiliating to think that by a peculiar circumstance, they have been given the right to tell us what we can see and hear. If they were willing to admit that their job is as hopeless as we have shown, we could feel some sympathy for them.

But, they like their work. They refuse to discuss it with prying reporters. They belong to the sequestered saintly. And they are not brilliant people. Misfits. Lawyers, doctors, and writers who failed to make good. After all, it is not an honourable job. It isn't something to boast about before a group of real men and women. And so they shut themselves up, they deny their futility, and they cling grimly to the once unimportant paragraph of legal phraseology that gives them a more arbitrary power over America's mass entertainment than the constitution allows its President.

It is the law, and not the personal genius

of the censor that makes him important, powerful, and pernicious. And he will grow more important. The industry itself will not, cannot, fight him.

THE HEAVENLY INFLUENCE

III

CENSORSHIP of the movies has been in existence for more than a decade, a period sufficient to permit of evaluations. We should expect to find that the large and famous producers had by this time ascertained just what their masters—the censors—would cut out. Surely Fox, Paramount, Warner Bros., et al., have learned long ago how to meet the standards of the censors and thus save hundreds of thousands of dollars of expense. But no such meeting of the minds is possible. The standards set by the censors are more unstable than quicksilver. Each censor has his own pet fears and horrors, and each state board views the

79

dangers of life differently. No two censors agree, and no two boards coincide in their judgment.

Once having accepted a program of pure objectivity and impartiality we would expect to find the problem of the censor very simple. But, although most fields of vital thought and controversy are removed from their realm of consideration, this does little more than magnify the petty problems still residing in the material submitted. The very narrowness of the area of art presented induces an exaggerated fastidiousness of decision, for the censors must find something to cut. If the movies produced during an entire year only the worst type of Pollyanna puritanism the scissors would not be put on the shelves. Men who are hired to cut would feel unfaithful to their tasks unless their trash baskets were full of clippings. Censors are human beings and it is inherent in the bestowal of power on man, that he uses and abuses it. He never resigns it.

At the outset of their dilemmas the censors present a divided front. In some cases the censor is content, no matter what the treatment

MR. EVAN CHESTERMAN. The kind but firm gentleman from Virginia who reported "business
better than ever!"

accorded, if only the crook is always caught and punished. He must never escape. The erring wife must suffer, the husband may not have an isolated jag; nothing short of a gutter sot satisfies the censor. Thus does he imagine that the audiences will become virtuous by precept and example. The erring wife may, in scenes up to the final debacle, appear as a happy soul, the drinking husband as a comic imbiber, and the thief as a gifted and clever navigator. But some censors lack full faith in the belief that the audiences will subscribe whole-heartedly to the adage that the penalty of sin is suffering. Possibly the censors know too well the unreality of such hypothesis. In such moods they still force the theme to be so clear that we can detect the villain from the start by his smirks and the heroine by her smocks.

In addition they watch each scene and caption to make sure that sympathy shall never flow to him who in the end is ruined. Possibly they fear that we of the audience may decide to purchase some such temporary joys, figuring out our own odds on getting caught. Maybe we believe that life, as lived at present, does

CENSOR CUTS OF 1928
INCLUDING CLASSIFICATIONS AND LEADING COMPANIES

CENSORS' CLASSIFICATIONS	EDUCATIONAL	FOX	METRO-GOLDWYN-MAYER	PARAMOUNT	PATHÉ	UNITED ARTISTS	UNIVERSAL	WARNER BROTHERS	FIRST NATIONAL	TOTALS
1—Portrayal of Crime	1	180	55	56	59	....	106	28	14	499
1A—Suicide—Reference to	....	....	....	....	....	....	....	....	17	17
2—Display of Dangerous Weapons	3	91	162	48	135	12	52	13	12	528
3—Cruelty—Brutality	2	19	53	56	52	16	52	16	10	276
4—Reference to Cruelty	3	20	15	18	46	23	15	5	5	150
5—Mean or Mischievous	3	16	24	8	25	3	16	3	6	104
6—Capital Punishment—Reference to	....	....	4	3	....	2	2	....	....	11

										TOTAL
7—Gambling	….	3	10	….	3	3	14	….	3	36
8—Profanity—Lip or Title	….	10	13	6	6	3	16	3	7	64
9—Drinking or Reference to	….	3	8	7	9	2	16	6	2	53
9A—Narcotics	….	….	….	….	….	….	….	….	….	….
10—Sex—Suggestive	….	13	90	163	117	89	8	30	99	509
11—Over-Passionate Love-Making	1	6	40	12	13	20	3	10	10	115
12—Nudity—Indecent Exposure	6	15	28	31	16	13	22	8	16	155
13—Vulgar Dancing	1	2	10	16	3	6	14	4	4	60
14—Improper Reference to Women	….	5	3	8	6	2	3	3	3	33
15—Derogatory Reference to Countries	3	2	18	6	3	3	11	….	4	50
15A—Derogatory Reference to Religion	….	3	2	4	….	….	5	2	….	16
16—Vulgarity	29	20	18	40	47	77	10	….	8	249
16A—Nose-Thumbing	1	3	10	7	2	….	7	3	2	35
17—Unclassified	….	….	….	….	….	….	….	….	….	….
TOTAL	53	411	563	389	542	274	372	134	222	2960

83

not always bring the true deserts of virtue. We may even have learned from our present civilization that wealth is at times the medium of exchange for safety, and that with money we can civically atone for anti-social acts.

The boards are inconsistent. What do they do?

The accompanying chart includes every movie reviewed by the state board of movie censors in 1928. The movies include every production made during the year by the companies named in the chart. By glancing at this chart you can see what really troubles the censors. (Newsreels are not included.) 579 feature movies were reviewed in 1928—only forty-two, despite the factory-precaution of the companies—passed untouched! In one or more states, forty-four were rejected, and in the balance 2960 cuts were ordered. These changes were either titles, captions, or portions of the films running from short shots to long scenes.

We will translate this chart into its various dominant ingredients but before doing so we call your attention to the god-like precision which the categories attempt to create. Apparently there are 17 deadly sins with four additional footnote sins, and we particularly call your attention to sin number 17: "unclassified." Such a word in connection with an administration of a criminal statute is nothing more than a pigeon-hole for all remaining prejudices and fears, and although 1928 left this space empty, the mere existence of the category shows a fanatic zeal for new fields to conquer. For the producers to contest such standards of the censors is to guess themselves into jail. Practically all of these titles, used to classify the cuts made by the censors, consist solely of phrases composed of weasel words. No two men can honestly agree on definitions of such captions and yet on the construction of words like "improper reference to women," "derogatory reference to countries" depends in the ultimate analysis the producer's freedom from jail. If we guess as best we can as to the meanings applied by the censors to these 21 categories we find that our condensed figures show that cuts were occasioned as follows:—

	Number	Percent of Total
Items involving crime.......................	1672	56.4%
Items involving sex...........................	872	29.5%
Items involving taste........................	348	11.8%
Items involving the government......	49	1.7%
Items involving religion..................	16	.6%

Of course, this kind of itemization is worth very little because who can tell whether "cruelty" (category classification number 3), relates to sex crime; and whether a portrayal of suicide (Number 1 A) is considered a reflection on the poverty allowed by our government, a sexual inversion or a criminal act.

We defy you to find any group of real men and women in the world who would consider these standards of morality as anything but a burlesque list of prohibitions. Pick up any magazine, any newspaper, any novel, and cut it according to these rules. Even half the advertisements would be cut! The censor pictures a world of ladies and gentlemen dammed by "Elsie Dinsmore" and sired by "Lord Fauntleroy." He cuts to hold his job—and in the whole preceding chapter not one cut showed the hand of consistency.

86

THE HEAVENLY INFLUENCE

The real conflicts arise when the censors treat specific problems. Foremost of these (in importance, if not in number of cuts), is the adjustment arising from the troubles of the two sexes. The increasing interest in life has, to be sure, led to greater uncertainties, and more apparent inconsistencies. But how absurd for the censors to set themselves up as high priests of morals at a time when our codes are still hit-and-miss. Although there are no real leaders to interpret the transient sex codes, even the children are developing sex curiosities of a more normal, natural and healthy sort. Out of a free exchange of thought on this important subject the next generation may be able to orient itself.

What do we see in the movies? Only a form of deadening static which spells stupidity. While he allows vulgarity and sickly sentiment, the censor manages to lay his hands on realism in the few good movies that come his way. The most artistic parts of "The Racket" and "The Patriot" were cut—because they hit home. What possible harm could Pennsylvanians receive from seeing Emil Jannings gallop through the corridors of his castle to see his mistress. The mistress was not cut—the story was unchanged—but the gallop could not go. It was funny. It was masculine. And the women and men of the Pennsylvania board resented it.

Why must the censors pervert Hawthorne's "The Scarlet Letter," Hardy's "Tess of the Durbervilles" and Tolstoy's "Anna Karenina"? Miscegenation being taboo, we find a ban on "Othello" and "All God's Chillun Got Wings." The theme of prostitution in "Damaged Goods" and "Mrs. Warren's Profession" makes their production impossible on the screen though open to the theatre. Do the censors deny the existence of adultery, abortion, infidelity, bastardy and divorce? Why cannot the movies treat of divorce? A serious problem; in New York State alone it creates an annual crop of 12,000 criminals (since adultery, the sole ground for divorce, is also a crime). The movies are censored to a condition where sex attractions must remain sheer romance, with mating the result of only heavenly influences. Not even the censors can be-

"The Barker." The creative work of the Pennsylvanians. This shot was unartistic, immoral, etc.

lieve that the sex drive of men and women can be drained off by seeing a couple marry under a caption: "They lived happily ever after."

Not a single Wagnerian opera can be screened. The voluptuousness of the opera presumably is harmless to the occupants of the Golden Horse Shoe, on the theory either that the rich are so corrupt that nothing can hurt them further or so pure that they are immune from sexual influences. But Tristram, Siegfried, the entire Niebelungen Ring are taboo in the movies.

In so far as all the censors unite in banning any true portrayals of matters sexual there is a uniformity of decisions. But beyond that point, in the area of treatment of detail we find a mass of ridiculous trifling editings all calculated to destroy what little there is of the genuine in the scenario itself. We have seen that some censors abhor a kiss on the neck; others fear the sight of a knee, while to some a hair pin is the symbol of sin. Much of this is on a par with Comstock's wild fury at seeing a dressmaker's bust-form in a show window.

89

PRIVATE LIFE OF THE MOVIE

The movie censor is rather pitiful in his urge to put us back in the ankle-and-bustle era, while sex books, sex lectures, and sex news surround his dingy office. But when it comes to crime he is merely a sad-eyed misfit hiding under the bleachers while the crowd above him roars at the show.

While the movies must doctor up all crime action, still allowing the public to know full well who kills whom, or how she was seduced, or how he was robbed, the Press prints pictures of the Tulip Garden, the ganders and the sporty auto of Peaches Browning, pages are filled with photos of the apple tree, the location of the bodies and the Parsonage all made famous in the Hall-Mills case; and the window sash in splendid enlargement perpetuates the glories of the Ruth Snyder-Judd Gray murder. Again, the censors and Will Hays boast of keeping politics out of the movies. No wonder we have so few movies that have lasted a decade. Can any art thrive on disinterestedness? Does not creative energy arise from partisanship? Was not Christ the greatest of partisans in his understanding of the

prostitute and his raid on the money lenders?
Look over the list of the great in literature!
Bacon, Locke, Addison, Goldsmith, Macaulay,
Mill, Gibbon, Spinoza, Dante, Moliere, Vol-
taire, Jefferson, Rousseau, Heine, Dumas, Zo-
la. These and their followers were aflame with
partisanship. These are the heroes of letters—
all, to be sure, on the Papal Index.

Despite President Hoover's request that the
citizenry obey all laws alike, the censors continue to believe in nullification, discrimina-
tion and even at times a blind faith in the sac-
rosanctity of law, hoping to make our body
of laws fixed and unchangeable.

The diversification of attitude on the liquor
question symbolizes the disintegration of the
censors' purposes. We have shown by chapter
and verse that in some communities the censors
remain unblushing when seeing a bootlegger's
dive, while in others any reflection on our
"noble experiment" is banned from the movie
no matter how far disrespect for Volsteadism
has become a fetish of a people resisting sump-
tuary laws.

In the main, our screen attitude toward

91

crime is coloured by a million dollar morality. Roulette wheels, cards and dice are usually cut from the pictures while the great American Gambling resort, the Stock Exchange, is reproduced with great pride. Torture as represented by capital punishment may not be portrayed even as a form of partisanship for abolition of state murder. At the same time the horrors of the Iron Maid, and the abysmal suffering of characters as in Ben Hur are continued in many pictures. Thus we see that the censors are selective sadists—bearing no grudge against evidence of man's bestiality, but merely directing its use.

Probably the most incongruous and illegal action ever taken by the censors was to bar Fatty Arbuckle from the films. No one need condone his notorious sexual escapade but surely the censors went far beyond the letter of the law when they banned pictures in which he acted. True enough, the public had some ground for outrage and complaint, but to the censor the sole test should have been within the four edges of the film. Does not the law relate to the effect of a picture? Canon Chase, the leading proponent of censorship, stated under oath that even Chaplin's influence was questionable. Are the censors to examine the morals of producers? What of the income tax scandals of many Hollywood stars and the divorce dilemma of many others? Should not the censors, if consistency is even a cheap jewel, look into the morals of all actors, actresses and even producers?

In order to gain a perspective on the censorship of crime movies it is interesting to speculate on how censorship would have reacted to the area of penal actions in previous days. Movie censorship in the days of the revolution would have helped perpetuate public street whippings, public hangings and the use of stocks. Pictures of the stealing of horses would have been allowed only if handled delicately, while stories of poachers could have been shown only by separate shots, one of the hunter with a gun jumping the stone fence and then another with the game in his bag. Disobedience to Sabbath laws, long since nullified, would have been among the strictest taboos. Wearing braided hair was at one time a crime

93

in Connecticut, and we can imagine the distress of the early 19th Century censor at the sight of ladies' tresses.

Conscription of men for war was illegal, and that practice, followed in 1917, would have been barred as an epitomy of illegal governmental tyranny. But possibly the movie censors appointed by the Crown would have been loyal to Great Britain and thus there would have been censored out of the movies all of the revolutionary spirit of the American patriots. At a later day when our country was part free and part slave, the Hays of the Civil War no doubt could have arranged for non-partisanship and the Lincoln-Douglas debate could never have reached the talkies, and "Uncle Tom's Cabin" would have found no counterpart in the screen.

Thus censorship might have operated in past eras, even though today some of the state boards have declared that these early developments of our national life are "so sacred that no scenario may treat historical events in a humorous manner."

If the movie censor could suppress the daily

news of the Sinclair and the Doheny trials, the utility investigations, he might exercise some influence on his subjects. As it is, he is merely expressing his own character by such fears. He does hold his job and keep the movie infantile. Those are the only benefits—if such —of his work.

After crime and sex (two very minor details of living) the censor seeks to preserve a Ladies' Aid attitude toward government.

Corrupt public officialdom is pictured only with mild and excusing scenes. The breakdown of our courts, decried by even Chief Justice Taft, is eliminated in a belief either that the press is unread, or that the press by endeavouring to procure reforms through exposure is acting unwisely. Imagine a scenario picturing a stupid or corrupt movie censor, and a good pure girl opposing such dishonest official. It is idle to believe that such scenes would be passed. What is more natural than that these numberless office holders should become sensitive to personal criticism and then use their power to block all reflections on their high offices?

And this prim regard for state is carried over to cloak the church. Many of the deletions arise from a desire to shield the *dominant* religious groups and the leading national minorities from insult or criticism.

Suppose a writer created a theme involving the effectiveness of the confessional as practised by the Roman Catholic Church, or the conversion of portions of the Methodist Church into lobbyists, or the relations of the Baptists to the theory that man sprang from monkey instead of mud? No such theme has ever been allowed on the screen. Whereas no one welcomes needless or cruel attacks on any group in the community, nevertheless we see no warrant even in law for the censors to set themselves up as the high priests of religious impartiality. Surely they are just meddling when they order that no clergymen may be shown attending the funeral of a crook, as they did in "The Racket," for even the lowest of us. is presumed to be welcomed at his death by some God. In "Potemkin" they banned a picture of Lenin's tomb bearing the inscription "Religion is the opiate of the People," igno-

DR. GEORGE HELLER. "Hair-tyer, jeweler, printer,
clothing-designer, druggist, doctor, censor."

rant of the fact that the respectable *New York Times* has printed the identical picture slogan on several occasions in its Sunday supplement.

This kind of interference not only stamps the movies as an adolescent nurse-girled mode of expression, but in fact is contrary to one of our national mainstays, the separation of Church and State. We had been led to believe that the State would not even by indirection be an aid to any religion, and that such a basic philosophy of government extends so far as to give equal treatment to a non-religionist. Surely the right to worship must carry with it the right to abstain from worship. But here again the censors inject themselves into the scenarios, for never is a finger raised to prevent criticism of an agnostic or atheist.

So far has this religious censorship gone that plays like "Abie's Irish Rose," and "The Merchant of Venice" can be movied only by extensive editing. Shaw's "Saint Joan," Ibsen's "Brand," Sinclair Lewis' "Elmer Gantry" are way beyond the pale.

They can only be read in book form or acted on the stage.

97

This ultra sensitivity to religion is paralleled by a desire for non-partisanship to national groups—at least the politically important ones.

Our censors some day may ban Gilbert and Sullivan's "Mikado" from the screen just as the English censor did from the stage, out of deference to a Japanese Ambassador. But these desires to be delicate with national feelings do not apply to Turks, Bulgarians, Liberians or others who have no vote. The negro can still be called "nigger," the Chinese "opium sniffers" and the Nicaraguan patriots "bandits."

But if you think the censors are far afield in this kind of interference you certainly must think them mad when you read the endless stories of censorship of mere matters of taste. If States change gradually, if religions pass through reforms, if nationalism rises and falls, if crimes are ever changing, certainly little mannerisms are so volatile as to be beyond human grasp. But to the censors Hell must be spelled H——, as if that kind of childishness fools anyone. We defy the censors to fill in the three blank spaces to form any other word that makes sense. *Since when did robustious-*

ness of speech or manner become a problem of the State? Are we unmindful of the Elizabethan drama and all of the classics that have become compulsory reading in high schools and colleges? Are the censors tyrannized by words and phrases?

All of these trifles of possibly poor taste which the censors delete have no possible relation to "good" or "evil." Most of us desire a life of taste and fineness of feeling, but aren't we better off with untrammeled films, working out their own solution as a result of direct reflexions of audience reception rather than through an ineffective smoke screen established by office-holders and nineteen-year-old volunteer maiden assistants? Aren't the great state governments stultifying themselves when they engage in expurgating water bottles and commodes? Moreover, all of these attempts to purge the films of unlawfulness, sex, irreligion and bad taste are not only ineffective, but evoke dangerous reflexes from the audiences.

If this is the level of taste to which the audience is directed by governmental mandate, obviously we have accepted officially a Gospel

99

of Tawdriness. If, on the other hand, the public leaves the theatres still shocked by the vulgarities of the screen then the censor is to blame. He has the power to reject any cheap movie you have ever seen.

Such are the social crimes of the censor. He damages an article costing $1,000,000 as his fancy chooses. Yet he himself is liable to no examination. Street car conductors, subway guards, pool-room proprietors, and soda jerkers have to pass some sort of examination. Does the censor pass an examination? He does not. He even has the authority to call some old spinster from a county seat and use her judgment to help him in his destruction! The censor is a political job-holder. A minor one. He is appointed by a ward boss, recommended to the governor. He may have some petty influence in his community. But as for the public—it seldom knows who he is.

His work is petty, but it keeps the movies sapless. He was given this power when the movie was a gawky infant gurgling to express itself. In those days actresses were humiliated to work in a movie—now movie stars conde-

100

scend to appear in person. In 1911, the days of the first laws, reputable authors dismissed the movie as garbage. Today they write stories and pray they will be made into movies. The talking movie has abducted the finest talent from Broadway.

All this time the movie censor has grown in power and severity. Each year he has cut more and more. The tax-payers, unaware of his existence, are helpless. The movies are afraid to fight—it might cost money for a month or so, and that month might spell ruin. The press has shown no interest.

You are probably helping to support one of these boards in your state. Certainly not one of them has a record to be envied by a real man or woman. If, with the Supreme Court of Ohio, you consider the movie devoid of ideas or drama, then this record will not disturb you. For your part, the movie belongs in the Church basement and on the library shelf alongside "Little Women," and the "Motor Boys."

But you cannot deny the existence of 20,000 movie houses, the work of a dozen great directors, and the existence of some famous actors in Hollywood.

And if you believe they should be given as free a reign as a magazine, a book publisher or an editor, you can well question the fact that your taxes in part support these boards of powerful intolerants.

The producers will do nothing. The press, weary of movie press-agentry, wary of movie advertising, will join in no protest. And the censor will not lay down his shears voluntarily. He has grown in power and usage. He has many friends. Chief of these is the club-woman.

LADIES AT PLAY

IV

IT IS a narrow projection room. The low hum of the movie machine and the mutters of five women alone break the silence. Lights! The women move into the conference room and solemnly mark their neat ballots—

"Good"

"Fair"

"Poor"

"Educational"

"Subversive to morality"

The National Board of Review is at work. Mrs. Hardy, from White Plains, thinks that it is subversive to morality because no good husband would poison his wife. Mrs. Schultz, whose husband is a Brooklyn chemist, sees no harm in the movie. Poison is hard to buy and easy to trace. If a husband is going to kill his mate, a poison scene in a movie wouldn't give him any new ideas, says Mr. Schultz. Mrs. Parton, (who left her children with a neighbour in the Bronx) sees no harm in the movie under consideration, but she thinks the opening scene is inartistic.

Hot goes the debate. Luncheon-time, and the women decide that, after all, the movie is harmless. The following afternoon the movie appears before a matinee audience of salesmen, shoppers, tourists and chorus boys with the respectable insignia "Passed By the National Board of Review."

In 1909 the People's Institute organized the National Board of Review. A political campaign threatened to wipe out the new nickelodeons. One of them was showing "The Great Thaw Trial." A publicity-hungry mayor ordered all movie houses closed. The stage managers were for it, the ministers wanted it—

104

even Mr. Thaw thought it was a good idea.
With a remarkably keen statement against
censorship, Charles Smith, of the People's Institute, organized the Board to save—not censor—the movie.

The Board was encouraged by the industry
in that the Motion Picture Patents Company
—then starting the still pugnacious fight for
movie control—felt the National Board could
give its product an odour of sanctity and respectability.

In its proclamations, the Board stoutly maintains the broad principle which Charles Smith
gave it. The following broadside is the Board's
own statement of its work.

"The basic work of the National Board is
the review of motion pictures which are submitted by the film companies producing and
distributing pictures before they are released
to the country at large . . . the Board reviews
from ninety-eight to 100% of all films. The
work is of an advisory, editorial nature, based
on its study of the psychological reactions
of motion picture audiences to what they
see." According to its own testimony, the Na-

tional Board of Review merely gives the producers suggestions based on the study their reviewing committees have made on the psychological reactions of the public.

The Board goes even further in declaring its non-censorship principles.

"The group of individuals composing the National Board of Review has been given no arbitrary power to regulate motion pictures," it says; "it is under the influence of no church organization with its well defined moral code. It finds its rule of practice in American common-sense."

Even better. A group of non-partisan critics, offering producers and public their suggestions. A safe theory, harmless and virtuous. But how is this done?

The Board is made up of:

1. A General Committee.
   A group of 25 people to which policies are taken. An advisory group.
2. Executive Committee.
   5 members. Has charge of money, memberships, all administration.
3. Membership Commttee.

Has charge of membership lists, recommends new
members.

7 members.

4   Reviewing Committee.

250 members. Does the actual reviewing in New
York offices of movie companies. Volunteers,
serving without pay. Over two-thirds feminine.

Obviously the *executive* and *reviewing* committees are the real workers in the organization. The executive committee is in charge of the entire work of the board. This work is:

1—Reviewing and advising.
2—Editing a magazine. Subscription $2.50 a year.
3—Selecting and advising Better Flims.
4—Issuing a Home Study free magazine.

The committee members serve without pay. The executive staff of five is paid. How much, they would not divulge.

Anybody may belong to the board. Expenses and salaries are paid by the movies, magazine subscriptions, and contributions from women's clubs. The actual reviewers, who mark the ballots, are not paid. They are women of New York City who apply for the job and are selected each week by the executive staff. For the most part they are middle-aged, non-professional. They see practically all movies, even before the state censors. However, as Mr. Barrett, head of the Board, admits: "No matter what we advise, the state censor will cut something. He has to—otherwise he loses his job."

The Board makes this statement to its creditors.

"The National Board was not created by the motion picture industry and is distinct in its operation and the conduct of its financial affairs."

This is pretty hard language when you consider that the Board earns a great part of its living by charging the producers $6.25 for every thousand feet of film, and that this charge brought them at least $75,000 last year. Besides, by getting permission to see films in advance, they are able to get out a monthly magazine of film reviews, for which they get $2.50 a subscription.

What is the Board's relationship to the movies? In one short paragraph we find it.

"The Board's first purpose was the pre-publicity inspection of films, which the producers agreed to submit to its members. A mutual

108

agreement was reached that when the Board, as a result of this inspection, asked for changes in part or total condemnation of films, *the producers would abide by its decisions, with the right to appeal to the board's general committee."* And there you have it. The Board announces that it is only an "advisory" outfit, that it merely recommends, but here you have it definitely stating that it has made the producers agree to *Censor* if the board so demands.

And with that sentence, you can dismiss all the high-sounding talk of recommendation as hooey of the first grade. The producers actually *pay* a "volunteer" reviewing committee, established by no law or vote of the public.

The executives of the National Board insist that they are merely a selective, and not a censorship organization. According to law, they are not. Practically, they are. As a matter of fact, Florida has a statute saying it will accept any movie "passed by the National Board of Review." In other words, if a movie was not passed by the Board, by law Florida could not accept it. And that smells like censorship.

109

PRIVATE LIFE OF THE MOVIE

The producers do not have to pay the National Board of Review a nickel. They do not have to abide by its decisions. Why do they pay then; allow pre-inspection? For the same reason the Chicago laundrymen pay the racketeers. For protection.

The National Board of Review is the biggest woman's club machine in the country. Four big groups with delegates, corresponding secretaries, all furiously writing and exhorting each other, contribute to the existence and maintenance of the National Board of Review. These four clubs are: The Daughters of the American Revolution; The International Catholic Alumnae; the Parent-Teachers Association and the General Federation of Women's Clubs.

However, even these four clubs have no legal power, such as Doctor Heller holds in his office. Why do the movies bother with them?

But you know the answer. When Will Hays took over the reputation of the movies and started to clothe it in shining raiment he found his main opponents in the women's clubs. He also found the National Board of Review in existence. He therefore took it under his wing like a good campaign manager. He uses the National Board as a female chorus for his cantata of movie purity. As a matter of fact, the producers do not completely abide by the Board's decision. As one executive remarked "when they object to a scene we go over and over it until, as a woman who has lost her virginity, the idea isn't so horrible."

Another executive said that the National Board of Review really had no influence, but that the movies—advised by Will Hays—kept all the organized women in one place so that they would not cause more trouble.

The active head of the National Board, a Mr. Barrett, is an intelligent and harassed man. He himself has no great Good to support. He brings two convincing arguments to support the existence of his board.

I—It does not censor movies, merely advises and recommends.

II—It is interested in "treatment" rather than subject matter.

We have two answers for him. In the first place, with the Florida statute in existence the

111

board is a censor, whether it wants to be or not.

The second answer is contained in the story of "An American Tragedy." Will Hays asked the National Board about it. The D. A. R. objected to its being made into a movie and Hays told his client not to make the film—it would cause trouble. Now the D. A. R. could not have told in advance what sort of treatment was to be used. Dr. Cadman might have played it—any director could have been hired. Obviously, they had read the book, heard that it was censored in Boston, and decided it was an unfit subject for dramatization.

"Now," says Mr. Barrett, "if the producer had made 'An American Tragedy' we would have passed it, but we could not have given it a recommendation!" In other words, because of the club-conscious Will Hays, the women's clubs gathered together by the Board are being given more power than even the Board's executive asks!

It is the old movie story. Fear. Fear of losing money. Fear—the Hays fear—of losing

112

the support of the Methodist and Presbyterian ladies.

We could agree to the theoretical advantages of the Board but common-sense and everyday occurrence deny them. Women who have nothing to do go to club meetings. Movie producers are a fearsome lot, they have banded together and given a politician almost arbitrary power, and with no feeling for real courage, taste, or dignity, he has allocated a censorship power to the ladies.

Your Associated Press has no group of women sitting in the news room cutting the stories. Your publisher has no group of twelve sitting in the composing room telling the boys what they can print. True, the ladies raise hell when some of the news comes out, but we have no objection to that. We do object to the fact that, not content with state censorship, Will Hays has allowed these club women to send delegates to Hollywood to "work" with his office on movies before they leave the factory, and that he takes the opinions of the D. A. R. and the rest of the ladies before you or I or the director

113

has a chance to have his say as to what is drama, art, news, or filth.

THE CLUB WOMAN'S CLUB

In 1920 we bounced back from a war. We were in an ecstatic state where no phrase was too large for us to hurl at the face of logic. We had saved the world for democracy. We injected war virus into the veins of the church and the organized reform groups and they turned savagely on us. Most violent and terrible in their revenge have been the women's clubs. And, unfortunately, it was in 1922 that the movie came out of the barn and began to travel in good society. Chaplin, it was discovered, was a great artist. Grudgingly, critics began to acknowledge the new art. But there were those who refused to accept this ubiquitous and insidious fellow. They resented his past. Chief of these uncompromising people were the club women.

Consider her rise, her age, her home town. Try to think of Indianapolis, Birmingham, Dallas in 1914. The Club Woman then had no
114

radio, no electric washing machine. She seldom went to the movies—the air was foul and the seats hard.

She went to club meetings where they discussed patterns, new canning recipes and their neighbours. Probably she joined the club when she had her second child, so she wouldn't "lose touch with things." She was thirty-two then. She is forty-seven now, and she is fighting militantly to keep hold of things that seem to change their colours like chameleons over night.

Her old grocer has been sent to jail for bootlegging. Chain stores have set out their prim signs. Local news has disappeared from the pages of her morning paper. She reads, with a yawn, the daily casualty list of violence on her home town streets, she reads a New York column and a serial novel.

Consider her home. She has a maid. She has a radio, and electrical appliances once reluctantly installed but now highly approved by the Club Women—even marketed by them at times.

Her youngest daughter wants to go to Cornell Med. and become a psychiatrist. She doesn't understand her daughter, who hasn't been inside a church for ten years, who fiercely repudiates the old religion, the old standards.

Here she is, forty-seven, no work to do in the home, no intellectual capacity for meeting even her daughter in conversation. Her husband works at the office, plays golf and goes to club meetings in his spare time. This woman has given birth to two children. She was *busy* then. She felt some relationship to life.

What can she do now?

Stuart Chase has given her a diagnosis. In "Men and Machines" he says: "There is one department where it seems to me that skill has been lost with no off-setting comparison. We have taken many of the housewife's tasks into the factory and left her to gossip, play bridge, buy more clothes than she needs and make a sad spectacle of herself at so-called culture clubs."

Consider her strength. She is a mother. She is a church worker. She is a respectable woman. She is a voter, a *worker*. And she is organized. Who are we, writers and tinkers, lawyers

116

and doctors, to fight her? It is a tough job. No politician—certainly not Alfred E. Smith, will deny that these women have power. But the politicians are able to direct that power easily; no man will say that politics has become purified in the last ten years.

The women are not powerful enough to beat the press, the publishers.

But the movie producer is taking no chances. He doesn't want to test their power. While he was doing it he would lose too much money.

A hundred producers might fight—a monopoly of ten must obtain a maximum sale—they cannot afford to fight.

And then there is sex. With venereal disease, violence and destruction stalking the streets of the country, there must be more than one reason why the club woman seeks to find a Utopia by subduing the movie. We have a good dozen male guilds that include the best scientists, the best minds of the land. The American Medical Association, The Bar Association—do you find them writing furiously to each other: "You should see 'Sunrise': there is a really dreadful

117

scene between a man and woman in a pasture" . . . ?

The movie is an art. As such, it has only the few chemicals of life to deal with. And the Club Woman is more interested in getting her hand into those chemicals than she is in really fighting the enemies of her world. Does she really worry over the future of our children? What they see three hours out of the week in a movie house is not nearly as dangerous as the stories of crime and graft their parents may discuss at the table, or the diseases they may contract because their parents feel it improper to discuss them at all.

No, the Club Woman, a middle-aged woman with nothing important to do, is looking for a vicarious experience with life. And through the courtesy of the producers, she can all but spank the torrid gals and send to the corner the big-eyed heroes of Hollywood when they are naughty.

If the owners of Hollywood wanted to find their worst enemy they would find him eating in their own kitchen—the press agent. Since a high-pressure orator sold Theda Bara, a very gentle and simple young lady, to the public as a modern Messalina, tales of lurid lives have filled the cheap newspapers and the movie fan magazines. Thus, while she takes the fan magazines and follows avidly the matrimonial career of her favourite star, the Club Woman has a breathless feeling that the women of the movies are all women of the world, and that the men are super-lovers. She can get a thrill from seeing and reading about it—but it might hurt her neighbours!

If a movie star commits suicide, it is news. If he is discovered crazy with dope, it is news. The press agent of 1920 has done his work. We all know that Hollywood is the one big bagnio, the one grove of Daphne allowed a stern and frigid nation. At least, the Club Woman knows it. The press agent told her.

But wait. It is 1929. Who *are* some of the present movie stars?

Walter Houston
Ruth Chatterton
H. B. Warner
Baclanova
George Bancroft

119

PRIVATE LIFE OF THE MOVIE

Daniel Haynes

Herr Bohmen

Al Jolson

Go over the list of talking stars. They came from the stages of the world. Your Barrymores, and your Baclanovas encountered no objections while they were on the stage—*but Hollywood means sex to the Club Woman.*

Remember the time—1920-22-24. The club woman has less and less to do at home. The movies are growing in strength. The press agents are using the old-fashioned sex lure to get a full house.

Now, in 1929, Wall Street greatly controls the movies. Playwrights and popular authors write them. Old-time troupers act them. Where is your sin? In the mind of the Club Woman. You can't fool her. The movie is wicked. She read about the Wallace Reid dope case.

As a matter of fact, no civilized man finds Hollywood an idealistic community. But, have the Club Women ever attacked the Shuberts, David Belasco, or the theatre, as they have the movies? No. No press agent ever told them about the lives the boys and girls lead. The

120

movies went on a publicity drunk. They sold their wares under the name of "sex." They are suffering from a severe hang-over. The Club Woman who sees four movies a week, cannot help but get a kick out of the idea that she has the power to keep the lid on Hollywood, the seething sex-poll of the world.

If state censorship were abolished it is possible that the Club Woman would stay within bounds and merely recommend movies to her group. But, with the National Board of Review reporting to Hays, and Hays whispering "caution" to the producers there seems to be no method in sight of diminishing the power of the Club Woman. She is growing mightier.

Last year she had twelve representatives sitting in Hollywood reporting to Colonel Joy, a Will Hays lieutenant. In theory, even this extraordinary vigilance might be harmless. In practice, it sets a disturbing precedent. We have no precedent in American letters allowing any group of women or men to see and pass judgment on news, literature or opinion before it reaches the public. It sounds like a petticoat autocracy, this movie business.

121

THE BISHOP OF HOLLYWOOD

V

IN 1919 Will Hays became interested in the movies. Several years before, a peace-provoking movie, "Civilization," had helped turn an election Democratic for Woodrow Wilson, and Republican-manager Hays was anxious to see that nothing of that kind should happen again. Quietly he set about meeting Zukor, Fox, and other potent movie men. Harding got in the newsreels, in the White House, and Hays was made Postmaster General.

In the fall of 1921 Roscoe Arbuckle gave a party in San Francisco and during the general merriment a young lady died. Several days later the fat comedian played his first tragic

part, and admitted that he had been the indirect cause of the girl's death.

It was hot news. The press agent already
had sold Hollywood to the customers as a blaz-
ing, wide-open den of sin. For the first time,
the customers felt they had seen inside the tent
into the real show, and they were ready to tear
up the stakes and run the carnival out of town,
in the grand old American manner. Clerics
ranted, Club Women panted, and the press
pointed with fear to the ripe bacchanalia of
Hollywood. More important, box office receipts dropped off. The big producers held a
conference. Baseball had ridden over a black
period by getting itself a bishop. Why not the
movies?

In 1922 Hays accepted an offer of $100,000
a year and became the head of the Motion Picture Producers and Distributors of America,
Inc.

To begin his work, Hays had to become a
super-press agent. Before him the little men
had cried "sin, sin" and the public had pushed
its nickels across the counter. But they had told
their story too well, and it was up to Hays to

123

cry "for shame—all is pure." And he did a good job. Whatever else he may be, he is probably America's greatest press agent.

Since 1922 Hays has grown in power and influence as his clients have developed. Now, instead of sending pleas of innocence to city editors, he confers with prime ministers. He is the most important man in the industry.

Consider what that means. So accustomed are we to sudden wealth and fantastic achievements we accept the most enormous ironies of living as everyday occurrences, as part of the cosmic scheme. Suppose a writer were called into conference of all the publishers in the country.

"We need a Czar," he is told. "We will give you $100,000 to help us out of this hole. We will take your advice, give you arbitrary power."

A million Samuel Butlers and Hardys, Poes and Cabells will toil to an old age before they are given such an offer.

Yet a medium more powerful, more influential than the novel, was practically turned over to one man in 1922. Suppose he had been

124

a great psychologist? If he agreed with Brill, he might reason thusly:

"Urban life has robbed its millions of the machinery of loving, hating, fighting, with which they were born. We shall have free movies for the masses to afford them a cheap Kartharsis, to prevent torch murders, and grim passions. We will teach biology in the movies. We will award prizes for the best movie of American life.

"We will give honourable mention to the finest movie architecture. We will fight poverty, war and venereal disease in schools with the movie." These, and many other things the doctor might prophesy.

But the movie was not given into the hands of a writer, a scientist, a statesman. It was turned over to a politician, a Presbyterian elder.

Will Hays was brought into the movie industry to give it the stamp of respectability, the atmosphere of conservative elegance, that characterized the Harding Administration. Since then his work has been in two over-lapping divisions: social, political.

125

PRIVATE LIFE OF THE MOVIE

He is the safety valve, the lobbyist, the soft-spoken voice in the ears of the mighty. He deals with movie censors. He settles trade disputes. He assuages the fears of the Club Woman, the foreign embassy.

Will Hays was employed, and is employed by the movies to make them money. There is nothing inherently wrong with that ancient idea. Unfortunately, the movie is a more animated and volatile thing than a tractor. By saving, or presuming to save the producer money, he has to work with dangerous materials.

In order to understand the perplexities of his position, think of the way the movie is sold.

Company A. makes movies. It has also 1200 theatres, and a controlling interest in two other large theatre chains. It sells movies to independent theatre owners—men who merely show, and do not make the product. Company A. sells its movies abroad. It owns a theatre in London, a chain of theatres in Germany. The domestic product is censored in six states, reviewed by the National Board. Censor cuts cost money. Before the movie leaves the fac-

126

tory it is practically in the hands of the Will Hays office. If Pennsylvania consistently hacks Company A.'s product, Hays must either get the gentlemen to listen to reason or show Company A. how to make movies that will get by. Company A. sends a movie to Germany. An under-secretary objects to scenes of American soldiers triumphing over the Kaiser's men. Word reaches Washington. Hays talks with the Ambassador. A compromise is reached. Company A. may make war movies but it must not show an American actually killing a German or vice versa.

This sort of thing goes on all the time. There was a tragic fire at the Cleveland Clinic caused by film gas. A government inspector demanded that movie warehouses increase their protective devices. Hays produced a chemist who testified that developed film produces no lethal gas. He saved his clients money. He watches Washington constantly for signs of repression. He works closely with the Department of Commerce. He settles trade disputes. He is ambassador to all foreign countries.

All movie companies do not subscribe to the

Hays office. Twenty-eight belong. They produce 90% of our movies. They control the biggest movie chains. If the independent theatre owner did not buy their movies he would starve to death. Without the aid of Hays a young movie outfit would find it hard to battle the censors, to understand and find ways of selling its product. Hays, and the Film Boards of Trade, arbitrate the constant fights between the theatre and the factory.

With his knowledge of politics, his influence, his skill, why doesn't Hays fight the censors? He does, and he doesn't. He fights new censorship bills, but his general policy has been to let well enough alone. His writers send reams of literature to the press praising the innocence of the modern movie. He seeks to eliminate censorship in this manner. As you will recall, Hays has not been noted in the past for putting his cards on the table.

Again, if he defied the censors it would cause trouble. The politicians would object, and Hays has a tender, forgiving spirit for the politician. The independent theatre owners might object to the dominance of the big producers, and Senator Norris or some other fiery liberal might bring up the old suits the Federal Trade Commission has brought against Paramount et al., and cause further unpleasantness. No, Hays will not start a street fight with Pennsylvania or Maryland censors. Rather he will caution his clients to take it easy.

Hays is not an actual dictator. He advised against "The Green Hat" and the producers went right ahead and made it. But, if they disobey him, they must take the consequences. On the whole they watch the reports that come into the studios every day from the Hays office listing the state cuts, and seek to find some indirect method of avoiding the censor's shears.

It is not strange that Hays should handle the censors so gently. Of course, he does not view the movie as an inorganic sales object. Neither does he feel it is an art that should be given the freedom of the artist's mind and hand. Somewhere he has found his definition of the movie. "Caution" is his pass word. Speaking of the movie's attitude toward youth, he said: "We must have toward that sacred thing,

129

the mind of a child, toward that clean and virgin thing, that unmarked slate—we must have toward that the same responsibility, the same care about the impression made upon it, that the most inspired teacher of youth would have on it."

Again, he postulated a movie rule. "We must protect the morons and see movies" . . . and concluded by saying that "the motion picture is the epitome of civilization." Certainly the history of the movie would indicate that it has been made for morons and youths.

However, the urge of the present power of the movies has taken Hays away from the actual business of censoring movies, and seeing that his clients stay in line. He has a shrewd and clever office force that does this work with a tongue-in-the-cheek attitude. Hays himself is really a corporation press agent. Once that was a simple business. Today it connotes all the guile of an international diplomatic service.

When Hays first started his barrage of purity broadsides he had one job: to cool the fires of the righteous. That job inevitably devel-

130

oped into an economic as well as a social assuaging machine. Ever since Ivy Lee took over the ghost of John D. Rockefeller and clothed it in the shining raiment of charity, finance has employed a so-called publicity department to say masses for its soul.

Every financial group has these contact men, priests administering rites to the consumer. The Petroleum Institute, the National Electric Light Association, the Neighbourhood Grocers, etc., etc. These guild press agents have two jobs of selling to do. One, to actually exert indirect selling methods; the other, to permeate the simple atmosphere of trade with a benign and sanctified Purpose. In other words, you are not asked to buy an electric refrigerator because it will keep the ginger ale cold, but because electricity is man's greatest work since the machine gun, because it is relieving man's burden.

You are not asked to buy an automobile as a means of conveyance, but because a few altruistic engineers worked in a monastery for nine years to perfect a convertible rumble seat. You are not advised to buy a cigarette because

131

it has good tobacco but because it will keep you slim, pure and exotic.

Hays is the biggest priest of them all. He not only has a huge corporate body to sell to the public, but he has a product that at any time may blow up, kick back, and hurt the owners. He has to be careful and virtuous. And he does a good job. All movie producers are not fools. They underestimate the assimilating power of the American middle-class, but they have no illusions as to why Hays is worth $150,000 and more a year. The old attitude that a movie executive was not far from the moral standards of a white slave operator still lurks in the minds of the press-agent believing public, the public of 1917. And Hays has taken the Club Woman, the church and the censor and humoured them enough to get their support. If his clients were not competitors, and if all the good directors would die or stop work from sheer nausea, he would be able to make the movies as clean as the editorials in the Sunday *Times*. As it is, they are pretty well under control.

Hays, the actual man, is not hard to locate.

THE BISHOP OF HOLLYWOOD

His career bears testimony to the real nature of his ambitions and ideals.

Born in Sullivan, Indiana in 1879, he became a politician before he was of age. The thin-legged, large-eared boy started to study Blackstone at the tender age of ten. He was admitted to the bar when he was twenty-one, having previously graduated from Wabash College. The year before he had been made a Republican precinct committeeman. In 1908 he had reached the offices of the State Committee. He practiced law in the firm of Hays & Hays and was active in Indiana politics in the Republican party for ten years. He was involved in the fantastic financial pastimes of the Harding administration. He has been with the movies since 1922.

He lives in the Ritz Tower, has offices in New York and Chicago and likes to pay flying visits to Sullivan to show the boys he is still a plain Indiana citizen, but he hates to stay very long doing it. He was divorced for incompatibility last year after twenty-seven years of married life. He is an omnivorous joiner. We list his clubs and past offices. Motion Picture Pro-

ducers and Distributors of America, Inc.,
1922; v. p. Nat. Bank of Sullivan; dir. Conti-
nental Baking Corpn.; Fletcher Am. Co., Indianapolis; Chicago & Eastern Ill. RR. Co.
Dir. Ch. and Drama Assn., Boy's Club Federation; v. p. Roosevelt Memorial Assn.; trustee
Inst. for Crippled and Disabled Men; mem.
Nat. Council Boy Scouts of America, Inc.;
Citizens Com. of Salvation Army; Am. Green
Cross; Am. and Indiana State Bar Assn. National Inst. Social Science; Acad. Political
Science, Phi Delta Theta (pres. for Ind. 6
years, Natl. pres. 1920-22); chmn. co-ordinat-
ing com. Am. Red Cross and Near East Re-
lief, by apptd. chmn. laymen com. Presbyn.
Bd. Ministerial Relief and Sustentation, May
17, 1923. Mason 32 degree, K. T. Shriner, K.
P., Elk, Loyal Order of Moose. Clubs: Uni-
versity, Columbia, Indianapolis Athletic, Sul-
livan Rotary, Indianapolis Country; Terre
Haute Country; Sullivan Country; Illinois
Athletic, Chicago Athletic, Hamilton, Indiana Soc. (Chicago); Metropolitan, Nat. Press,
University (Washington, D. C.); Chevy
Chase (Md.); Union League, Nat. Republi-

can, Bankers, Army and Navy, Friars, Advertising Embassy, Hudson River Country (New York) ; Hollywood Athletic, Kiawanis (Calif.) ; Vermejo (Colo.) ; Mayfair. Home: Sullivan, Ind. Office: Sherman Bldg., Sullivan, Ind.; and 469-5th Avenue, New York.

A man used to the ways of political subterfuge, with no especial literary or scientific background, Will Hays peculiarly epitomizes the class-conscious, fearful yet aggressive spirit that has made the American movie an industry, and little else. Search hard and find a man more fitted to handle petty politicians, middle-aged meddling prudes, and aggressive financiers. The controllers, the movie barons, are satisfied with his work. The dividends are coming in. We can expect no fight for freedom, taste or mature thought in their product so long as the Bishop of Hollywood chants his platitudes and swings his pot of purity.

135

THE ARGUMENT FOR THE PURE

VI

THE NATIONALISTS

ALTHOUGH the mere itemization of the cuts made by the censors as shown in the previous chapters and the roll call of the censors themselves are sufficient to condemn for most people this kind of governmental restraint, there nevertheless remain some few persons who argue that the objectionable features of our present censorship arise solely from a lack of uniformity. Men like Canon Chase urge that if censorship is not working today the sole reason for the failure lies in the fact that we have failed to enact a nation-wide uniform censorship law. He would abolish the state lines and he would concentrate censorship in

THE ARGUMENT FOR THE PURE

Washington. The answer to such a stand must be approached from two angles; in the first place, is this breaking-down of state lines consistent with our national tradition? In the second place, what kind of national censorship law has been proposed in our Federal Congress?

If we had remained a land of only 800,000 square miles, increased facilities of communication and travel might have produced a uniformity of civilization between the lumbermen of Maine and the cotton planters of Virginia. But we now cover five times the expanse of land and even the radio and aeroplane have failed to destroy the manifold distinctive variations that lead the folk of the Western Plains to exchange a mutual scorn with the apartment house dwellers of Manhattan.

One of the great attributes of our life is the ability of each of the 48 States to continue with its own pattern. There is a constant cry for National uniformity, and in so far as our 120,-000,000 people have arrived at an ultimate and final standard there is slight objection thereto. Thus we have uniform bills of lading and

137

other slight technical instruments that raise insignificant, if any, reasons for variation dependent on the multitude of customs of our different states.

But there are still many who wish to standardize everything in the Nation. It was thus that the National Prohibition Law was established even for the dry lands. At this time, with our divorce laws in a horrible mess and resting on local hypocrisies it is urged that a National Law will cure the ills. But what would a National Law give us in such a field, the Reno provision of short residence and great concern for the nervous state of the wife, the New York statute resting solely on adultery or the Carolina Law which forbids divorce even in cases of insanity? Would we not standardize down to some stupid level and then find such national law irrevocable as in the case of Volsteadism?

Such comparative collateral considerations should underlie any examination of a National Moving Picture Censorship Law, such as has been urged by the puritans and introduced into Congress. We must admit with Canon Chase,

138

the leader of the censors, that the states that have censors differ in their codes, that cities disagree with states and that the bulk of the Nation are living "without Benefit of Censor." But is there any virtue in having an entire nation whipped into a national lock step? Who will determine the pace of the march of the 120,000,000 robots? Even if censorship had any merit, would we not be better off suffering under the inconsistencies of state censor boards than under the tyranny of rules as to morals and education laid down by a handful in Washington?

In 1928 there was introduced one of the most amazing documents ever printed in this land —a bill to create a Federal Motion Picture Commission. The framers do not use the word "censorship," because they hope that the public won't see through this insidious measure. But under this bill the Secretary of the Interior becomes a High Censor and appoints six petty censors—each with a petty salary of $9000 a year.

But these high priests of the land are told just what to do. Page after page is filled with instructions to these censors—and not one sentence is definite and clear. No wonder the vice societies backing the measure indicated that even Calvin Coolidge would not meet the high standards required for a position on the Commission!

Section 22 orders the commissioners to cut anything they deem "unpatriotic," or which will portray "distorted or untruthful representations of our national life, literature, manners and customs." That surely is some order! Would a scene of a labour union strike, the Sinclair Oil trial, the Charleston dancers, the stock exchange, be truthful representations of our national life? But coupled with this mandate, that varies with each individual's background and prejudices, the bill proceeds to say that no movie may hold up to "scorn" any "race, nation, sect or religion." Out go most of Ibsen, much of Shaw, and surely Shakespeare's "Merchant of Venice."

Are our faiths so slim that they need this kind of protection?

But if this kind of control—more extreme than any known in the history of any nation

140

but Russia and Italy—does not condemn the measure, let us look just one step further. No pictures aiming to assist the election or defeat of any political candidate shall be exhibited in licensed places of amusement! What of our rights as free men to have the talkies replace the old town meeting house and the gatherings on the Commons? Just when will the talkies have to omit remarks of the President of the United States: a day, a week or a year before a coming election?

After creating a dull stupidity for all movies, preventing them from touching any of the vital issues of the people, the censors then have to refuse licenses for any picture:

Which "emphasizes sex appeal"—let us try "Romeo and Juliet."

Which shows a "cock fight"—but bayonet killing is allowed and appeals for a big navy are not to be banned.

Which shows the horrors of White Slavery, even if the picture is developed by reformers to end that pernicious trade, or:—

Which makes an illicit love affair "prominent," shows persons scantily dressed, or contains unnecessarily prolonged expressions of passionate love. Here then we will have to install a meter with a sex voltage test. Such National censorship would spell only corruption and nullification. Do we want to start bootleggers of movies?

But these vice hunters are eager and bitter. Their proposed law provides that gambling cannot be shown if attractive, and the stories and scenes must be so constructed that even the morally feeble "may not receive an emphasis on crime." Thus all adults are to be censored to the level of the feeble-minded. No tyrant of past ages ever tried to go so far.

But that is not all. We may not ridicule or deprecate public officials. This is nothing but a tyrant's creed. Who are these officials but our servants? Haven't we increased the public corruption of this era by failing promptly to criticize and deprecate our Fallses and Forbeses and ridicule our drinking but dry-voting Senators? Good government rests in part on the right to ridicule unfaithful governors.

The next paragraph of the act prevents anything which may offend the religious belief of

142

any person, creed or sect, or ridicule any clergyman. Since when are church and state reunited in this country? Why shouldn't we ridicule, if we feel like it, the clergy—as we do the flapper?

And so does this lunatic measure read on and on for page after page. These $9000 a year censors must cut out anything "vulgar," or partaking of an improper "gesture" or "attitude." Our every motion is to be standardized.

Were it not for the fact that the busybodies of the land are organized, the movie producers uncourageous and the balance of the public disorganized and disinterested, this kind of proposed legislation would be unworthy of comment. But we cannot be unmindful of the step which produced National Prohibition and the distress occasioned by the impress of a National Law on an un-nationalized people.

A National moving picture censorship law would endeavour to develop a static civilization without variations in taste or thought, thus denying the wisdom portrayed by President Wilson when he declared that: "The function of all education was to make the young men as much un-like their fathers as possible." A National censorship law is not the answer to the incompetent and bewildered work of the state censor boards.

A LITTLE CHILD SHALL LEAD US

There is one other argument raised at times in favour of censorship despite all the evidence that can be produced as to the insanity and inanity of the workings of censorship to-day. There are some people who know the evidence we have set forth but remark—"Of course censorship does not work at present; we have applied an insufficient dose. We must multiply our boards and increase the number of deletions. We must cut until it hurts; then only can we obtain the pure screen which will protect the children of the land."

Before addressing ourselves to such an extreme attitude we must briefly refer to the legislation already enacted affecting the relation of children to movies. About 10,000 children in the United States, under seventeen years of age, weekly pay their tribute to the screen. Mr.

144

THE ARGUMENT FOR THE PURE

Hays estimates that 8% of the urban audiences are children. Forty states have no regulation whatsoever. Children unaccompanied may witness any picture any time of day or night without restriction. Only two states have really definite statutes—New York and New Jersey, where children under sixteen may only go to movies if accompanied by parent, guardian or authorized adult. Six other states, New Hampshire, Massachusetts, Connecticut, Rhode Island, Michigan and Mississippi, prohibit admission of minors during school hours and after certain hours in the evening.

Thus we see that practically outside of New England children are not dealt with separately by the states, but it is assumed that the parents have the prime right to control the destinies of their own offspring. The six states with partial regulation apparently are concerned solely with problems of truancy, or as in Oregon provide a sort of curfew movie law for children—9 o'clock in the winter, 10 o'clock in the summer. In these states the age limits vary from ten in Mississippi to sixteen for girls and fourteen for boys in Connecticut.

145

This latter variation can hardly be explained by the feminist movement.

The New York and New Jersey laws are not enforced. In the Survey of May 15, 1929, Roy F. Woodbury, a student of this very problem, makes the flat statement:

"To prohibit children from attending motion picture shows altogether is not the right answer. They will go in spite of this law and in fact it only creates disrespect for law on their part. Because the law is so inflexible there is a general apathy on the part of the public to its rigid enforcements. This is especially true in New York. There is ample proof that the laws in New York and New Jersey are openly violated."

Of course states like Maryland and Pennsylvania, where censorship is quite elaborate, need never be concerned about the children. Presumably all impurities have been removed by the censors, but New York and New Jersey typify the constant and age-long struggle as to domination of the next generation. The former struggle of church against parent has shifted to State against parent.

146

THE ARGUMENT FOR THE PURE

By and large, little real planning has been done in this realm. Obviously not every film is of value to every child. Surely a sage parent will try to direct his child only to those movies that are consistent with the balance of the child's development. Not every child remains unscathed by "custard pie" vulgarity. The pre-adolescent may not be entirely unmarred by doses of sentimental unrealistic approaches between the sexes. The children of the rich may even leave the theatre with not even subconscious receptions of the undue glorifications of wealth and the speciously high gospels of Mammon.

But the problem of child education via movies is not essentially different than with other media. Geometry should not be taught before multiplication, or sailing before swimming. Precocious stimulation is to be avoided nearly as much as retarded instruction. The problem of modern education is mighty, but the movies —irrespective of their imputed potency—are negligible factors compared to other cheaper and handier influences. On every street corner in every land the child can buy for 2 cents

147

without restriction enough tabloid sadism and sexual perversion to fill up all his night dreams and day fantasies. Nigh-nudity—if that's a danger—is on the beaches for the adolescent—in flesh and life, and not only in one dimension on a flat screen.

Our modern attitude has abandoned the former psychology of national silence and taboo. Rather do we build up a next generation fully informed; not merely coated with half truths that create sordid curiosities.

Surely the unreality of the screens, as censored, surely the evasions practised to meet the censors, create situations leading to sneaky whispers among unliberated children. It is like showing children a picture of the human body with the genital organs removed!

Abroad, children are prohibited from attending performances unless special provisions have been made for showing specially selected pictures in special theatres, chosen because of safety.

Such a course has at least the warranties of an underlying scheme. Under such a policy producers in time may develop special pictures for children—the possibilities of which must delight every parent and teacher. But in addition to that high hope the counterpart of that type of protection for children spells freedom of the art for adults. The cry for censorship then should end; surely no one ever met an adult who declared that he wanted some other adult to act as his censor. With the children saved we need no politicians to worry about saving our souls.

Now, censors—because of the absence of child-movie controls, must cut their celluloid to fit the lowest intelligence test.

With this child audience as an objective, is it any wonder that the movies—aside from mechanical development—have stood still? Scenarios still portray right as being the opposite of wrong. The movies deal with Good and Evil as parallel lines that never meet. Mr. Hays himself has spoken as the oracle of this unreality—

"There is no difference of opinion among decent people as to what is right and what is wrong in motion pictures or in anything else.

149

All the world over men's minds are much alike."

Is it any wonder that "the American film has served," as John Gould Fletcher in the *Crisis of the Film* has said, "as propaganda for the emotional monotony, the naive morality, the sham luxury, the haphazard etiquette and the grotesque exaggeration of the comic, the sentimental and the acrobatic that are so common in the United States."

It may well be as many educators contend, that movies cannot hurt children and can only act as an escape from drabness. In fact, Dr. Blanchard of the Philadelphia Child Guidance Clinic testifies that—"Numerous studies made by scientists have failed to establish any appreciable contribution to delinquency from motion pictures but we do find the motion pictures to be helpful in many ways."

But how about the adult—must he continue to be fed pictures with morals only in black and white? What can be more untrue to life? Where in real life do we meet the movie type of problem—clear cut, with undiluted good or bad? To feed adults on such falsity surely

150

must create embarrassments in real life, where the facts involving any decision or any act are never all on one side of the argument. Surely Hamilton's sexual indiscretions do not damn him in toto, any more than Washington's love for rum or Jefferson's ownership of slaves made them villains.

In their zeal to make life simple for the child audience, the producers, bending the knee to the censors, have created fantastic characters, living in realistic settings but untrue to real flesh and blood. Crime, lust and dishonesty are always in evidence as counterparts to virtue, asceticism and integrity. The censors reject the essence of true living, clinging to a tattered philosophy of free will. They wish the audience to be schooled in the belief that each one of us by Will Power alone can lead the "Good Life." What a despicable view of living! By its measure every case of the fall of man from his highest ambitions is due to isolated, unadulterated Will Power. Such a creed is nearly as vicious as the outworn dogma of Fatalism, which going to the other extreme indicates the absence of Will Power, and predicates all our steps and missteps on a Power in the Stars or Heavens.

Are we not ready for acceptance of the life of determinism? Are we not agreed that life itself, with its inescapable heredity and environment enmeshes us all at times beyond the powers of Free Will, or the holocausts of Heavenly Fatalisms? Do not the great dramas of life involve the suffering and frustration of human beings through no immediate fault of their own? Must the movies deny that life crowds us all, and that even the Censors—pleasant fellows at times—are only yearners for power and seekers of smut, because of hereditary or early environmental influences?

Censorship of the films twists the movies to meet the child's simple chart of life. To bring up adults on such distortions is to cripple emotionally the entire population.

THE URGE FOR GOOD

VII

THE EXISTING method of movie repression is insufferably stupid. A variation or extension of that method would prove only more vicious. Theoretically, a vigorous dredging might again open the channels of opinion and expression. Actually, there seems no unity of feeling or power among the citizenry capable of doing the job.

It is no new cycle in American politics. We have slid down to such ignominy every century since we took possession of the Indians' home. There is only one hope. Each slide has been followed by a painful and laborious ascent.

PRIVATE LIFE OF THE MOVIE

Although the vitality of this current era is renovating our previous concepts of religion, nevertheless the present urges of mankind, conscious or subconscious, are still traceable to what might genetically be termed a biblical background. And if we turn to Genesis we find that the third act of God in relation to Man was a mandate of Censorship. The first act was the formation of man, the second was to put the man into the Garden of Eden and the third reads:

"And the Lord God commanded the man saying 'Of every tree of the Garden thou mayest freely eat:

" 'But of the tree of the knowledge of good and evil, Thou shalt not eat of it: for in the day that thou eatest thereof thou shall surely die.' "

This mandate against treating life as a great experience and a thrilling accumulation of experiments was no doubt inspired by those ancient Hebrew authors who suffered from a supreme human failing—a yearning for the status quo. Man, it seems, in his mad obsession for power over others, has always feared

154

that shifts in thought would decrease the stabilities of life and increase the difficulties of adjusting to the new morals and ideas.

The history of civilization is little more than man's reaching for the tree of knowledge, his eating of good and evil fruits in such proportions as to create an organism capable of digesting the evil. Those who said: "Keep away from the fruit of knowledge—stay pure at the risk of staying dumb," brought on the very battles against the early Christians, the Inquisitions of the ages and all of the other tortures developed in the conflicts between those who feared the experiences of life and those who felt that life must be fully experienced no matter what the perils.

To keep the common people from eating of the tree of knowledge, governments have fought and crumbled. The printing press brought up new fears; and the Anglo-Saxon struggle for freedom of the press is one of the brightest records in our history. Printing a page of type required a license in England until 1694.

All during that time the stage in England

155

was thoroughly censored as it still is today. Except for a short period when Queen Elizabeth lifted the ban (which period brought forth the greatest of all English language drama) a writer of plays has had to submit his manuscript to an appointee of the Crown. Such officers carried the indicative titles of "Lord of Misrule," and later "Master of Revels." To this arbiter of public morals every pageant was submitted in advance. He then decided whether or not it was "moral, educational and harmless."

It is difficult to explain the complacency of the Britishers in submitting even today to this kind of control. Historically, the situation developed because actors were vagabonds, and theatres were scenes of possible riotous behaviour. The continued existence of this censorship proves the difficulties of liberating thought from the control of other men, if once such power is conceded and continued for some years. The protest of practically all the English men and women of letters has failed to influence the British cabinet officers who have

156

all read, but too easily forgotten, the famous words of Milton's "Areopagitca."

When the spirit of our Revolution was arising in the thirteen Colonies much of the hatred against the rule of King George was engendered by the endeavour of the Royalists to control the printing presses of this land.

Every school boy must be familiar with the attempts to suppress the early patriots. The assaults on Benjamin Franklin, and the incarceration of his brother James in 1722 by the Crown Government show the lengths to which the censors of those days feared the spread of ideas they deemed "harmful" and "immoral." Hundreds of printers were jailed for rebellion against the pre-censorship of the press. The signers of the Declaration of Independence are a roll call of the minute men of Freedom from the Censor.

Chapters out of our early history add further to the conclusion that we are betraying our founders.

When the Constitution of the United States was being written the question of postal censorship arose for discussion and George Wash-

ington urged the abolition of all stamps and
postal charges for fear that if fees were levied
for carrying the mails some kind of control of
printed matter might sneak upon us. Even
Alexander Hamilton, the arch reactionary of
his period, joined with Thomas Jefferson in
favouring such freedom of thought and communication.

When the Constitution was fully written
with its twenty-six separate sections, it contained no Bill of Rights, not one word guaran-
teeing freedom of thought and speech. But this
very omission makes doubly striking the special separate amendments carried only three
years later, in 1791, known as the Bill of
Rights. The first of these reads:

"Congress shall make no law respecting an
establishment of religion, or prohibiting the
free exercise thereof; or abridging the freedom of speech, or of the press; or the right of
the people peaceably to assemble, and to peti-
tion the Government for a redress of griev-
ances."

It cannot therefore be urged that this famous doctrine was merely part of an elaborate

158

instrument dealing with hundreds of other governmental exigencies. It had the separate isolated consideration of the people of the land.

In fact, a long view of the annals of governments leads many historians to believe that aside from the theory of States Rights, that is, the existence of forty-eight separate experimental laboratories, this enunciation of Freedom is our greatest contribution to governmental history.

But such victories as that of 1791 can never be held without constant vigilance. By 1836 serious attempts were made to give the Postmaster the right to censor the mails and to ban what he deemed injurious; the abolitionist literature of the North was disseminating into the South ideas which the slave owners deemed "immoral, uneducational, harmful" and certainly far from "amusing." But Clay, Calhoun and Webster with the deciding vote of Vice President Van Buren kept us temporarily in our path of freedom and tolerance. Not for long. In 1868 we started on the breaking down of our Bill of Rights.

It was then that Comstockery really started.

159

From that time on the Post Office has increasingly become a negation of the spirit of Benjamin Franklin—the first Postmaster General of the United States.

This letting down of the bars was induced in part by the accepted idea that ordinary criminal statutes against indecency were unenforceable. The machinery of justice functioned only after great delays, and juries would not stand for curtailments of liberty of the mails, which a single censor in Washington could order by his solitary mandate. The American people more and more have fallen into the easy acceptance of pre-censorship; stopping ideas in advance of publication rather than submitting to the constitutional right of court procedure. The inability of prosecutors to obtain convictions under the Volstead law led to padlocks —a form of law by injunctions, a method of penalty without trial by jury, a system of censorship by judges rather than convictions by juries. To defeat the will of the people, as enunciated by juries of the common run of men, those in power always have turned to control by one man censorship. The workers

of the land are suffering from the same un-
democratic fallacies, elucidated by thousands
of judge-made injunctions restraining the organization of unions and the right to cooperate
to raise the standards of life.

This was the mood of our law "givers"
when the brothers Lumiere, toward the close
of the 19th Century, perfected the motion picture camera. It was then considered an amusing toy—only a hundred yards could be taken
at a sitting. The old bioscope was a feeble
thing to fight a censorship which already controlled the Post Office, and against which the
workers of the land in the then industrial strug-
gles were impotent.

Movies of Broncho Billy and the original
Western thrillers cost trifling sums to create.
Even in 1920 the cost of a picture was less
than $150,000, whereas now the major pro-
ductions run over a million dollars a piece.
It was natural that the censors in the community would, as usual, attack the young, the
new and the weak. Every new art of expression is a dangerous influence against conservative society.

161

While the attack of moralists and censors was thus invited, the other side of the medallion showed a deplorable condition. The first owners of the industry were enrolled largely from the garment trades. Movies were just another business. That pictures dealt in ideas and emotions meant little to them. They weren't even "showmen," with pride in their productions. They were near bankruptcy time and again. They hated each other with a guerilla temper. A gang warfare ensued. The contest over patents consumed the energies of the owners. The movies were in a Racket.

Ramsay's authoritative study tells a tale of wrecked machines and stark struggle that left no time for watching the type of product or preparing for the army of the censors. And just before Wall Street commenced to stabilize the cinema industry the war came on with its hysterias, and further breakdown of constitutional protections.

Illegal deportations, unwarranted banning of pacifist periodicals, gagging of those who felt the war would lead to naught, persecution of conscientious objectors, were the order of

162

the day. If the test of a constitution is the strain it can bear in tumultuous times our own experience of 1917-1918 is none too satisfactory.

This era of suppressions and restrictions could not come to a dead halt on Armistice night. The gospel of war intolerance evidenced itself promptly in blue laws, anti-evolution laws, suppression of hundreds of books in Boston and elsewhere, banning of world classics by the Customs officials and padlocks on speakeasies. We became so censorious that these shores, long an asylum for political refugees, denied admittance to those beaten and tortured by foreign tyrants.

Without a philosophy of freedom, with no training in the concepts of Jefferson and Franklin, how could we expect the movie owners to organize and present a united front against those worthies who declared that the film was a tree of knowledge, and that man should by law be prevented from eating the fruit?

But who composed this army of forbidders! The blue noses were a few individuals falsely claiming to represent all the people of the land.

Women's Clubs, Home Study Clubs, Get Together Clubs, Literary Societies, Law and Order Societies, Federations of Church Women, Missionary Societies, Daughters of the American Revolution—forgetting their ancestry—joined in a crusade. This was to be expected. The industrial machine age had removed the housewife from her homely duties. Weaving went into the mills and food producing into the canning factories. War had given them new corpuscles. The only outlet for women was reforming. Their creative libidos, their zeal for control, turned to the control of mankind in general, which included the saving of souls by movie censorship.

These leaders of organizations claimed to speak for thousands and tens of thousands. James N. Rosenberg, in an address to the Bar Association of the City of New York, in 1926, presented an incisive picture of these casually appointed spokesmen of the land. "Mrs. Bowley represented fifty mothers; Mrs. Hart 40,000 members of religious organizations."

164

"The list," he says, "puts Homer's catalogue of ships to shame."

Thus the movement spread with the usual mob momentum of our indigenous capacity for organization through societies. In this land we are being governed by these clamouring societies, which in the lobbies of our legislative halls shout like majorities in the absence of authentic roll calls. Our objection is not directed against organized expression of opinion but to the dishonesties and ignorances which raise these articulate masses to a position which the real facts would seldom warrant.

It was to be expected that the movie magnates would become alarmed by the array of these women. How could Mr. Zukor, Mr. Lasky or Mr. Loew know that these women were not really potent delegates? How could they, ignorant of the histories of past suppressions, call a halt to this astounding repression?

With the industry as it was in 1915 there was slight hope for liberty. But even then the owners of the movies might well have relied on the Supreme Court of the United States to back them. Surely the First Amendment to the

165

Constitution and similar provisions of State constitutions had some meaning—pre-censorship such as we have pictured it in the earlier chapters of this book would be declared unconstitutional and the state laws would be voided.

In 1912 the Board of Aldermen of New York City passed a movie censorship ordinance. It came before Mayor Gaynor. The movie owners, if they had taken time from worrying about their theory of giving the public what it wanted, might have read these stirring words setting forth the Mayor's veto:

"It has hitherto been the understanding in this country that no censorship can be established by law to decide in advance what may or may not be lawfully printed or published. Ours is a government of free speech and a free press. This is the cornerstone of free government. The phrase, 'the press,' includes all methods of expression by writing or pictures. In past ages there were censorships to decide what might be published or even believed.

166

THE URGE FOR GOOD

The few were very anxious not to give freedom of speech or of the press. They thought the many were not fit for it. But in the course of time censorship and all interference with freedom of speech, of the press and of opinion began to give way until in the end they were abolished. There seem to be a few who wish to retrace our steps and resort to censorship again in advance of publication. Do they know that censorships of past ages did immeasurably more harm than good? If this ordinance be legal then a similar ordinance in respect of the newspaper and the theatres generally, would be legal. . . . Once revive censorship and there is no telling how far we may carry it."

But the owners of the Films had no Franklin in their industry. They were content merely to exist. And so in 1913 Ohio and Kansas enacted those censorship laws which in 1915 reached the highest court of the land for interpretation. How was the court to hurdle the Bill of Rights? Surely pre-censorship in this land could only be adopted by the use of ingenious and circuitous reasoning. But the Court found the way by relying not on the initial concept of our government but by admitting that court decisions are merely a confirmation of what the judges think is the common-sense of the community at that time. The Court said:

> "The argument is wrong or strained which extends the guaranties of free opinion and speech to the multitudinous shows which are advertised on the billboards of our cities. The judicial sense supporting the common-sense of the country is against the contention."

Thus movies were held to have no relation to dissemination of thought or emotions. The court stamped the Films as a business, an industry, not connected with art or ideas. Mind you, they went so far as to carry this position into the realm of news reels, and captions. The movies, the courts held, were barren spectacles unrelated to "sentiments," for the Ohio Constitution, redeclaring our Federal Bill of Rights, stated that: "Every citizen may freely speak,

168

write and *publish his sentiments on all subjects."*

The owners of the industry had treated it merely as a business, unrelated to social effect, and the Court took this clue and declared that the movies were another area like the Post Offices where the free and open market in ideas no longer prevailed. It was no answer to the Court to point out that practically every state in the Union had Indecency Laws on the Statute books and that under such laws the showing of an illegal picture could be prosecuted in the courts before jurors. The Court went beyond the constitution and wiping out the Bill of Rights said Pre-Censorship of Movies would stand because people at that time did not want freedom of the movies.

This arena which we have found from the time of Brothers Lumiere until 1922 carried unequal protagonists, packed audiences and indifferent defenders. Up to that time the tide was definite and running flood. When Alfred E. Smith, Governor of New York State, signed the bill creating a Motion Picture Censorship Commission the liberty of movies seemed lost forever. But the tide has been at ebb for some years. Not that the reformers ceased their mighty battle; but no new law has been passed in any one of the still free forty-one states. The record shows the following attempts at censorship, all defeated:

Year	No. of Bills Introduced and Defeated.
1922	3
1923	18
1924	2
1925	14
1926	2
1927	9

Even the Internationl Conference on Indecency, called by France (amusing as that may seem) under the aegis of the League of Nations, in 1923, came to naught.

The best proof of the turn is Massachusetts where, in 1922, after the legislature had passed a Movie Censorship Bill, the people of the State by a vote of 553,000, to 208,000, rejected the measure. This was one of five separate referenda put up to the people at that time and although the people voted down state liquor enforcement by only 100,000 they rejected movie censorship by 344,000.

Calvin Coolidge came out flatly against a Federal Interstate Censorship bill in 1926. If Dr. Wilson had so spoken in 1915 the Supreme Court might not have reached the opinion that the common-sense of the people supported censorship of the films.

Since 1922 no state legislation for censorship has been possible. The hosts of Canon Chase can make no headway against movie fans. But a new power, a new control has climbed into the saddle. And legislatures and the public have been hanging to the stirrups. The urge for good has passed out of the pulpit. It now permeates the conference room. In ten years, a new economic power, an undreamed of master, has employed the simple fears and the ancient tools of the censor. At a time when prudery and propaganda seem worn to a thin fabric, a new power has stepped in to give life and strength to the powers of darkness. It is the corporation.

THE PLAY'S THE THING

VIII

NEXT TO fighting and loving, our chief diversion since we crawled out of the caves has been playing. Once as simple as the ecstatic dance of aboriginal tribes, as unrestrained as a midnight gallop of a wild horse troop, we began to harness that exurberance of spirits to a trumpet, a piece of cat gut, a tablet of stone or the smooth side of a cliff. Instead of beating our neighbours over the head with clubs when they failed to see the wisdom of our ways, we took them aside and urged logic upon them. Fighters and workers whiled away their moments listening to the sad songs of the travelling minstrel. Even kings turned from their

172

favourite diversion to hear the worldly comments of their jesters. The artist, the critic, the professional player was accepted by society.

The professional player, living by virtue of the tolerance and endowment of his rulers, suffers with the economic and social condition of his state. The jester may hit too close home, and be crucified, stoned or exiled. The painter may too well show us the sick and diseased, and lose his license for existence by our displeasure. But the cycle of life has always carried with it a contingent of these peculiar men, writing large the history of our struggle with our environment.

The recording and creating instinct of the artist has not changed. Love, life, hate and death are his chemicals. He may work new forms, new compositions with them, but his ultimate aim, his desire for perfection in illusion has remained constant through monarchical, feudal, and democratic states of society. A Sargent or a Bellows did not discover new human aspirations or conceive them in a manner unknown to Da Vinci and Rubens. Bergson and Russell have not evolved a phi-

173

losophy of spiritual freedom unrelated to Socrates or Plato. Two thousand years of war and calamity have brought no intrinsic change in man's life. We have the machine, but it is employed to clothe, feed and house us. We have, possibly, less poverty, more wealth, more bodily comfort. But we have not yet destroyed poverty, eliminated disease or hate from man's life. We have lessened or heightened their activity, but they are still with us.

The Twentieth Century has brought only one real change in the old association of the artist, the critic, the patron. It is a complex, a disturbing, change. The movie, a medium of light and shadows incorporating the form of painting and the stage, is now America's fifth *industry*. Not even the later Greeks boasted of more than a minority devoted to playing. Yet we have produced an art responsible for the livelihood of millions and the entertainment of tens of millions.

This condition has brought about the new change of attitude. The artist is still an artist. The critic is still the interpreter. The patron has changed. No longer is he an aristocrat, a

174

Duke Sforza, a Francis the First. He is a commoner, a stockholder, a clerk responsible only to directors.

Movie control is being unified. The companies taking charge are, compared to the old patron, lifeless, inorganic machines. Not one man, two men, or a dozen are buying work for themselves. They are hiring men to turn out a sales item. And if censorship means more sales, and, incidentally, cheaper, childish movies, they are for censorship.

We cannot confine ourselves to the old values of the true critic. Economics and politics have scattered them to the winds. We must employ economics as well as criticism to determine the potentialities of the American movie.

Cause: the clumsy child of organization, the corporation. We have two serious and possible effects: (1) the return of pre-censorship for the stage: (2) the death of political opinion and the right of free speech.

The United States has become a body of corporations surrounded by land. In 1911 the movies consisted of a dinky projection machine and a handful of nervous fur workers. In or-

175

der to show you what their machine will look like in 1940 we have to perform an autopsy on the body of the corporation. Now we are not discussing men, but machines.

Food, steel, automobiles and movies are produced by corporations. After the war, the public utilities of this country needed millions for equipment. They got them by selling non-voting stock to a wealthy and propagandized public. Utilities needed millions for operating expense. Control began to gather in local, state, and national organizations. The holding company came into existence.

A few men with a genius for such organization have become extraordinarily proficient at this geometrical progression game. Following the lead of the utilities, banks, cigar stores, restaurants—every form of business—has become infected with this gregarious urge. Now the director, the controller of this machine is, in most cases, a responsible man. Responsible —to his stockholders. His companies must make money. When money is the sole consideration of a man his life narrows down—when

176

it is the soul of a company, the area is even more limited.

The director may be a man like Matthew Brush, with a hobby for elephants; or Wrigley, with a passion for swimming and baseball. But his company may have no such habits. It might mean delinquent dividends. Few of us today can escape contact with the corporation. If you read a newspaper, eat a shrimp, or buy a pair of pajamas, it probably bears a corporation stamp. General Electric employs 77,000 men. General Motors fifty thousand more. And these workers pay for movies, and buy radios made by other corporations controlled, in some measure, by their own employers.

If two men edit a paper, it is likely to have a policy malicious to at least a minority. But when two hundred men direct corporations controlling a hundred papers, or ten million radios, or 40% of the world's movies—and with the sole thought of making their companies show a profit—you can wonder how far the modern leader has run from Horace Greeley, Tom Paine, or Jefferson.

We have found a huge fear cloud shadowing the movie factory. If that factory was unrelated to politics, war, or even news, we could dismiss the cloud and say "it is not important." But the foremen of that factory have brothers and cousins in charge of machinery that runs our modern world.

We cannot indict this group of men personally. If they were ghouls, train robbers, cannibals—then we could dramatize them, and dismiss their machine. But they are not sheer black. They are merely control-men; sublimating their personalities to run machines fed by a public with which they have no contact, and about which they know but little. The movie is one of the biggest engines. They are using it to run things once considered individual property.

THE TALKIES

You may curse the groanings of the talkies or you may consider them the advent of an art as potential as Gutenberg's awkward press. Whatever the opinion of the public the producers regard them as movies. They have not

178

called upon the Shaws, O'Caseys or O'Neills of the theatre, they have not produced controversial or thought-provoking drama—merely movies "with sound."

In 1929 and 1930 the biggest movies were adapted from stage plays. Glance over the list:

Coquette

Constant Wife

Broadway

Burlesque

Front Page

Little Accident

Interference

On Trial

Trial of Mary Dugan

Thousands of people saw these plays without complaining to the police. *Not one play reached the movies without being changed in advance by the Hays office, or censored by a state board after release. And not one movie corporation made a real fight against this violation.*

February 4th, 1929, the Supreme Court of Pennsylvania decreed that its movie censor board could censor talking movies. We have seen that board in action. Needless to point out, a play with any political, social, or moral rebellion in it hasn't a prayer in Pennsylvania.

Of course, we would hardly expect to find the producers fighting censorship in 1929 when they have accepted ignominiously this condition ever since the industry started. The playwrights and actors hired away from the theatre usually enter Hollywood with a "what-the-hell, it's the movies" attitude, so one can expect no protest from them. It is the customer who receives the insult, the emasculated reproduction of drama.

There are those who delight in the awkward state of the talkies, and hold that censorship and mechanical imperfections will make the talkies so obnoxious the public will flock to the theatre. "Garbage" they call the movies. Very well, consider the heap, and analyze the stench. Not artistically, as some minor critics have cried, but financially, the talking movies are poisoning the theatre.

THE PLAY'S THE THING

THE STAGE

Broadway is the American theatre. Producers, actors, writers, all work within its drab environs. Today not one so-called legitimate theatre on Broadway houses a play! They show talking movies. Reason: the movies own the theatres. They own such reputable and famous old firms as Daniel Frohman. They have movieized such famous theatres as The Globe.

Therefore, with the American theatre, in so far as talent and theatres go, almost completely in the hands of the film corporations, censorship of the stage—which has never been attempted in open legal form since the American Revolution—is now at the door. The intelligentsia can look out of their windows and see the garbage truck unloading on their front doorstep.

We are genuinely sorry for the few real patrons of the theatre. Never an easy career, they are up against stiff opposition.

It is possible that 1932 will make it impossible for "An American Tragedy" or a "What

181

Price Glory" to reach the footlights without submitting to pre-censorship. It will be a real fight. Right now, we see no way of halting the progress of movie control and the logical step from censorship of dialogue on the screen to dialogue on the stage. A Supreme Court has made it easy.

Already the forces of censorship have taken courage from the rout of the movies. In 1928, the Wales Act was passed in New York State, the physical home of the American Theatre. By this law, a theatre owner may lose his license *for a year*, if found guilty of showing an immoral play. Almost all theatres are owned or controlled by the movies. But even an independent owner has to think twice before risking a court decision by showing a controversial play. It might mean a dark theatre and an empty pocket for a year.

THE RADIO

Not only is censorship preying upon the nation's fifth industry—because it is an industry and not a patronized art—not only are the meddlers taking a side entrance into the theatre, but they have been given recognition by a medium of news even younger than the movie. Here, too, it is the stockholder who is to blame. Not an aristocrat, but the men in charge of these great oracles.

The Radio Corporation of America is the radio giant of the country. We don't have to fumble for proof here. This offspring of the inventor and the corporation put on a muzzle before it got out of swaddling clothes. We list only a few incidents in which reasonable objection to political or social progress was censored by the Radio Corporation or its relatives.

April, 1926, station WEAF refused to permit Norman Thomas to speak on behalf of the United Parents Association because one paragraph of his speech which dealt with military training in high schools was considered "controversial matter." As a result of this refusal by the National Broadcasting Company, Station WMCA invited him to speak on "Freedom of the Air" and withdrew its invitation the morning of the day during which the speech was to be delivered.

PRIVATE LIFE OF THE MOVIE

The same month, Eamon De Valera was barred from delivering an address by KOA Denver, Colorado (General Electric), because members of the station's censorship committee decided at the last moment that part of his speech contained "propaganda against the British government."

April 20, 1927, Jed Harris, producer of "Spread Eagle" (a vigorous drama of the fermentation of a Latin-American revolution) was invited to speak over the air by WEAF and then excluded because of objections from the American Legion and other organizations.

Hudson Maxim, talking against prohibition, was allowed to talk into a naked microphone. It was cut off unbeknown to him.

In Springfield, a professor from Smith College, speaking on the foreign policies attitude of this nation toward the Near East, came to the station with his speech and the broadcasting company said "you must cut out the last two paragraphs and insert these two which we have written."

Editor Kaltenborn, representing a conservative Brooklyn newspaper supporting the Republican party, criticized over the air one policy of that party, and a station tied up with the broadcasting station promptly advised him that there would be no further time for him.

As a matter of fact, the air is pre-censored by the government. There are only a few wave lengths possible, and the Radio Commission has sole power to license broadcasting stations. We need hardly point out that the most powerful stations are not in the hands of anti-Methodist, anti-Republican or any rebellious groups. The Radio Corporation and the General Electric Company rule the air. Not one of a hundred patrons of art, beauty, free speech or easy living, but corporations. Responsible to stockholders. If you bought Radio stock at par, you can rest content. If you objected to the Nicaraguan invasion, you'll have to object at home. You can't put it on the air.

Now this censorship was not dictated by a $2,500 a year petty politician clinging to an old, outworn statute, but by one of the greatest corporations in the world. Thus we find our great corporate bodies assuming the same hypocritical attitude toward life as Censor

185

Knapp—not in ignorance but from fear. Fear of losing money, a majority respect.

Consider the evil. We can fight a politician. We need real strength to battle the financial powers of the world. Consider the omniscience of this control, this censored, sapless regard for life.

See where our playing has led us. The play is no longer a diversion, it is our bread-maker, thought-dictator, our ruler.

"The movies," declares Mr. Hays, "have never engaged in politics." There may be a change. Should there be, Mr. Hays hardly could be ranked as a novice.

The utility corporations and their affiliated financial groups are gradually acquiring a hold on the movies. The companies not controlled by the utilities are merging for strength and protection.

The Radio Corporation of America controls the R. C. A. Photophone. It controls the old Keith Orpheum chain of theatres. It has a producing company, Radio Pictures. Lock, stock and barrel it is in the movie business. And if R. C. A. would not let a man speak on

186

the Nicaraguan invasion over the radio, surely it would not give him a chance in a news reel.

The other movie giants are banding together. They depend on Western Electric, Vitaphone, or some utility-controlled device, for talking machinery. Financially, the utilities have the rule of the movies.

What are they going to do with it?

Consolidation demands greater production. Greater production means no experimenting, no dissension—maximum sale. We have seen that censorship already is employed by R. C. A. Movies of entertainment, obviously, will be turned over to our old friends, the censors. A fight would hurt the sale. Radio Pictures have been in business two years, and they have yet to protest against censorship.

And their political power becomes a real question.

TELEVISION

Eighteen million homes in the U. S. are wired for electricity.

Ten million radio sets have been sold.

187

PRIVATE LIFE OF THE MOVIE

The Radio Corporation and brother giants are in the movie business. Radio Pictures have purchased several big music houses, they have an interest in the Victor Talking Machine Company. Comes television, and the war is on!

Television will cripple the movie companies just as the talking movies have crippled the theatre. It will cut down attendance, and force the movies to give entertainment better than that furnished by the air. The point is, one great control will be able to colour news, opinion and politics before it reaches the great mass of people. If there comes a war, who will tell us the truth? We haven't yet learned what the shooting was about in 1917. We'll be called upon to polish up the muskets and start all over again—and one great giant will have the power to say over the air, in the theatre, "yes" or "no."

If you have regarded the censor, the Club Woman, and Hays, the press agent, isolated and unimportant influences in our national life, now, perhaps, you can see a design and symmetry moulded by economic circumstances. The puritanical zeal of the censor, the money-

188

mania of the producer, the sanctimonious odours of the Hays office all find their places in the great corridors of America's utilities.

They have gone into the movie business. They control the air. They soon will control television. Their muzzling influence has even extended to the press.

THE PRESS

We quote testimony presented in "Electric Utilities."

E. B. Hofer & Sons, of Salem, Oregon, received $84,000 a year for four years for sending utility propaganda in a news service they furnished 14,000 small newspapers.

College professors, Club Women and legislators have been hired to make "studies" showing the advantages of private control of utilities.

An estimated $28,000,000 a year is spent by the utilities in this benign advertising work!

The chain store has made the chain newspaper possible. Once a paper depended upon local subscribers and local stores for its existence. It simply expressed, contradicted or reflected the opinion of the community it served. Advertising is the life of the modern paper and magazine. A chain store has no actual contact with the community. Its owner does not lunch with the local minister. He sits in lower Broadway. The local newspaper is being bought by syndicates, simply because the syndicate can get the chain store advertising, publish the paper at a lower cost.

We do not have to go into this thing too deeply to recognize a familiar symptom of the new economic order. When the Post Office Department, in 1835, told Horace Greeley he must stop sending his newspaper to Lynchburg, Virginia, he simply wrote back and said: "I refuse to do anything of the kind." We wish a few of those old thunderers were back. Today, if the Post Office Department told a chain newspaper editor to discontinue editorials in a Southern branch, think what would happen. The chain store corporation, caring nothing for the situation, might say: "Your editorials will hurt our business. We'll

190

cancel our advertising if you don't stop it."
In 1930, it is hard to believe that the newspaper man would say: "I refuse to do anything
of the kind."

We do not say that freedom of the press is
as extinct as the dodo but common-sense would
prove that it is on the wane.

There was nothing actually insidious in the
fact the I. P. & P., a paper and power company, bought millions of dollars' worth of
newspaper stock in 1929. But common-sense
denies the idea, that if the fight over utility
ownership reached the press, the fact that a
power corporation was a big stockholder
would not influence the policy of a newspaper
chain. It isn't human nature to bite the hand
that feeds you; especially when it's a caviar
diet.

We cannot say that newspapers are censored
or controlled by huge corporations. We do say
that, corporations themselves, and feeding off
other corporations, the newspaper editor of today is shackled and silenced to a point un-
thought of by Greeley.

191

PRIVATE LIFE OF THE MOVIE

Movies, talking movies, newspapers, radio, music houses, gramophones, television—all indirectly or actually controlled by interlocked financial interests. That is the situation. At its best, in these days of ease, this control produces a universally cheap and prudish entertainment. At its worst, it has the power to actually dictate opinion to a nation, once called a democracy.

We see no reason for a reign of terror. The movies are in an uneasy financial situation. If urban crowds found beer easier to get or found some new form of entertainment (although we cannot think of such a one) the big movie houses might well be filled with empty pews. But whatever the future of this bloated corporate body, these facts remain:

1 A newspaper editor today hasn't the freedom granted in 1835.

2 It costs more to produce a play today than it did in 1925—the dangers of censorship are greater.

3 The air is controlled and censored by a few individuals.

You may call that democracy or progress.

192

Our wealth, our producing urge has brought us to this epitome of control.

We find no Beelzebub, no fiend to blame for this increasing and humiliating suffocation of personal liberty. If we could point to Adolph Zukor or Gerard Swope, and say: "He's the man, he murders children, maims innocent women, and shackles free men!" we could start a fight in no time. As a matter of fact, these fortune-builders are not evil men as were the old power monarchs, the mill owners of the Nineteenth Century. You would be perfectly safe in giving your child or your fortune into their personal protection. It is their system that is pernicious.

These men are bound to protect their companies, to increase production. Any deviation from the movies of the leading political party or the leading church means trouble. And trouble cuts down sale. Theirs is a simple formula. Unfortunately, they are selling us politics, wars, and government as well as refrigerators and airplanes.

There is some hope and some despair in the uncertain future. Mass production has created

193

superficial mass prosperity. Mass prosperity demands mass entertainment. In supplying the hunger the control group has severely crippled the theatre and practically killed the untried movie. The theatre and the movie will stretch their legs in little theatres, in art colonies. Meantime the power men feed their workers, their consumers on pap. Emulating the old, old idea of the English governors they say "keep them dumb." Cheap movies, cheap music, and cheap politics will satiate the mass for the time being. History monotonously swings its pendulum. If only they had the courage, the whimsy of the real aristocrats, the patrons of fine lace, painting and music, they could really pacify their yeomen. The American is no fool. The movie bores him, so he drinks gin. The radio irritates him, so he takes his neighbour's wife. Organization eventually will suffocate him, and he will start breaking the machinery. Unhappy, violent, yet bored, middle class America is capable of any rebellion. And all the mergers in the world will not purge it.

The bigots, the fools, the parasites have different desires, but they join with the control

194

men in curbing our personal liberty. The fanatic is amusing and supporting himself by reform. He at least has the virtue of ignorance. The corporation leader is deliberately shutting his eyes, cheapening his own culture, and trafficking in garbage, for the sake of greater dividends.

Search hard, and find a duller group of monarchs. Have you ever heard a radio announcer satirize a radio announcer? If they would let every radical, every hothead in the world say his piece, the power men could give us a good show and, well-fed, we would say: "It's so much hooey." Let them put the screws on and we say: "There must be something in it."

It is horrible to consider these men, stodgily endeavouring to keep us pure, honest and dumb. Unbelievably drab. If only one would go slighty mad, put on a good show, thumb his nose at the world, make us laugh! A king might. A director would be kicked out of the company and sent to a psychopathic ward.

We can have a grudging admiration for the old machine-builders who could get up and

195

say, "To hell with the public." The new corporation whispers, "God bless the public." We are just boys and girls together, working for the Great Good.

We could even submit to financial bureaucracy if it would let us make our own wars, and have fun in our own way. But when they give us ready-made Gods, fresh from the factory, and antiseptic, ready-made recreation, it is time to start throwing things and to exercise the Elizabethan prerogative of flogging ham actors. Humourless and dull, the power man and the censor join in trying to persuade us that George Washington was a cleric, Thomas Jefferson a Methodist and Warren G. Harding a priest. It isn't good enough, gentlemen.

Starting with Emma Viets and concluding with the board of directors of the Radio Corporation of America, we have a Utopia of moral and political beneficence set up and imposed upon a citizenry who do not deserve it, who do not belong in it. We have dropped a curtain upon the Eighteenth Century scene of America. It seems to have no connection with the present farce.

196

THE PLAY'S THE THING

The show is not over, and there will be plenty of action before the final curtain. 1930, however, brings us to a serious and unhealthy condition. The tinkering, harmless inventor and the meddling reformer have built a high-geared machine. We have licked the reformer again and again, but this time the gutless machine-owner is giving him a free ride on the steam roller. We can do one or two things. Get out of the way, or wreck the roller.

EPILOGUE

As you enter the main room you catch the warm glow of shaded lights. To the rear of the huge central room, you see shirt-sleeved men minutely observing the polished and intricate machinery of the control room. Your feet sink deeply into the luxury of the floor, and the quiet group of well-dressed middle-aged men and women seated about the microphone seem lost in the immensity and the magnificence of the decorations. It is a broadcasting station. Time: 1940. One of the men rises to his feet and scuttles noiselessly to the microphone. He is slightly bald and nervous. He leans toward the blank mouth of the air and announces in a carefully-restrained voice:

"Through the courtesy of the Amalgamated International Electric Company and Associated News Bureaus, the Congress of the United States announces to its citizens that today it

198

has declared war against Russia, Africa and Ireland."

The announcer steps back to wipe his pale brow. There is a flutter of excitement among the listening group. Two women clap their palms neatly.

"By courtesy of The Associated Food Company, the Universal Chain Stores and Associated Advertisers, the Marine Band will now play 'The Star Spangled Banner.' "

The Marine Band is switched to the air by the shirt-sleeved men, and 35,000,000 television sets quiver to the stirring refrain. Progress has declared another war to end war.